PIRATES AND PICKLED HEADS

AN ECLECTIC COLLECTION OF SCOTTISH SEA STORIES

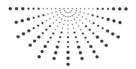

HELEN SUSAN SWIFT

Copyright (C) 2019 Helen Susan Swift

Layout design and Copyright (C) 2019 by Next Chapter

Published 2019 by Reality Plus – A Next Chapter Imprint

Edited by Fading Street Services

Cover art by Cover Mint

This book is a work of fiction. Names, characters, places, and incidents are the product of the author's imagination or are used fictitiously. Any resemblance to actual events, locales, or persons, living or dead, is purely coincidental.

All rights reserved. No part of this book may be reproduced or transmitted in any form or by any means, electronic or mechanical, including photocopying, recording, or by any information storage and retrieval system, without the author's permission.

CONTENTS

Introduction   v

Section I
THE PERSONALITIES

The Warrior   3
The Clipper Captain   14
The Southern Explorer   29
The Northern Explorer   38
The Island Monarch   50
The Father   57
The Admiral   69
The Alien   83
The Privateer   93
The Harbourmaster   108
The Seawoman   112
The Greenlandman   119
The dutiful   128

Section II
THE VESSELS

The Strong Ship   139
The Mystery Ship   151
The Fishing Boat   156
The Perilous Boats   163

The Legend	170
The Treasure Carrier	178
The Clipper	186
The Tragic	194
The Slave Ship	207

Section III
THE PLACES

The Claiming of Rona	215
Sprats, Stake Nets, and Smugglers	223
A Bell, A Rover, and A North Sea Graveyard	232

Section IV
THE PIRATES

Highland Galleys and a Pirate Earl	245
Cogs, Caravels, and Pickled Heads	260
Nautical Wooing and Kismuil's Galley	272
Pirates of the Hebrides	286
Scottish Pirates	306
Barbary Corsairs and Clydeside Privateers	317
The Last Hurrah—Revolution and a Chinese Scotsman	330
Epilogue	336
Dear Reader	337
You might also like	339

INTRODUCTION

Scotland has an intimate connection with the sea. Such a fact is not surprising as she has a mainland coastline of over 6,000 miles, and another 4,000 miles of island coast, compared to a land border with England of only 108 miles. Indeed, given that the southern land border was often closed through bloody war, historical Scotland was nearly an island nation.

From before recorded history, people have arrived in what is now Scotland by water, either as colonists or invaders. Roman galleys pulled past her coasts, the Gaels crossed from Ireland with the sword and the cross, while Norsemen brought fire, slaughter, and their superbly flexible longships from which evolved the Hebridean birlinn. English warships blockaded the coast and sometimes fell

INTRODUCTION

victim to their Scottish counterparts. Pirates eased out from Scottish harbours on the west and east coast while whaling ships dared the frozen north, and traders crossed and recrossed the North Sea and headed south and west across the Atlantic and to all points beyond.

Scottish trade with the Baltic, the Netherlands, and France extends back at least to the Middle Ages, and from the seventeenth century, Scottish ships began to probe beyond European waters. The French sought out Scottish shipbuilding skills in the thirteenth century, and by the nineteenth, Scotland was building much of the world's shipping. From the great *Michael*, the flagship of King James IV, to *Cutty Sark* and the stupendous *Queen Elizabeth*, Scotland created some of the finest ships ever to kiss the sea.

Dundee was the world's greatest jute city and Europe's most important whaling port, Aberdeen dominated the trawling industry, Leith was Scotland's royal port while Glasgow was Scotland's busiest. By the nineteenth century, men from the Northern Isles and the Hebrides were found in every ocean in the world. Scottish fishermen have scoured the seas from Greenland to the Bay of Biscay and from the White Sea to the Scillies, with herring ports such as Wick, Anstruther, and Stornoway amongst the most active in Europe.

Given this background, it is hardly surprising

INTRODUCTION

that Scotland should produce a plethora of maritime personalities and nautical stories. From her ports came adventurers and explorers, warriors and traders, smugglers and fishermen. All have had stories to tell, but most have been lost over time. Some, however, have been retained, either by accident or through deliberate recording. This small book recounts only a very few of Scotland's tales of the sea.

The book is set out in four sections. Section one covers some Scottish maritime personalities, warriors, explorers, an admiral, and a couple of lesser known, but equally interesting, people. Section two highlights some Scottish ships, and ships with a Scottish connection. Section three gives the often-neglected story of a few maritime places and section four highlights the piratical side of Scottish seafaring. The stories and articles within each section are standalone pieces. They are not in chronological order, but only placed as chance and my own instincts decided. The concentration on the east coast is purely because I was working there.

All in all, this book has no intention of appearing academic. Instead, it is an introduction to some aspects of the Scottish experience with the sea.

SECTION I
THE PERSONALITIES

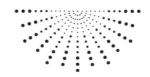

The sea is a hard mistress and serving her creates hard men. The sea off Scotland is particularly brutal, with frequent storms, an iron-bound coast and waters that can vary from freezing to merely bitterly cold. As the east coast faces Europe, each port there has a long history of trade, while the Northern Isles, with their long association with Norway, have supplied some of the best seamen in the world to British ships. The west coast, with its ragged indentations and scattered islands, lived by the breath of the Atlantic Ocean and produced a race of maritime warriors unknown anywhere else in Scotland. One such was Somerled.

THE WARRIOR

SOMERLED

They struck the Celtic coasts first, their dragon ships spewing the terrors of rape and pillage, slavery and murder on undefended villages and holy sites so that monks prayed for help. 'From the wrath of the Northmen, good Lord deliver us.' But there was little deliverance in the dark ages when Thor's hammer descended on the Cross. Time and the gloss of Hollywood have removed most of the horror that the Hebrides endured when the Norse arrived, but to the people living under the scourge, there was no romance. A chain of relatively small, sparsely populated islands set on the sea-road between Scandinavia and the rich monasteries of Ireland, the Hebrides were a natural staging point and target, with the holy island of Iona a prize for any grasping Viking with a long sword and a short conscience. Some of the reality of the Norse experience can be ascertained by the words of Bjorn Cripplehand, court poet of Magnus Barelegs, who described that Norse king's expedition to the Western Isles:

> *The hungry battle-birds were filled*
> *In Skye with blood of foemen*
>   *killed,*
> *And wolves of Tiree's lonely shore*
> *Dyed red their hairy jaws in gore*
> *The men of Mull were tired of*
>   *flight;*
> *The Scottish foemen would not*
>   *fight*
> *And many an island-girl's wail*
> *Was heard as through the isles we*
>   *sail.*

These words contain a jubilant acceptance of terror, violence, and death, but while half of Western Europe cringed beneath the iron seamen of the North, and Arabs and Byzantines learned to fear the swordsmen of Odin, the people of Scotland did not submit tamely to the invader. Scottish history books often concentrate on resistance to English aggression, yet the Norse were equally merciless and occupied more of Scotland, and for a more extended period, than any Plantagenet or Tudor king. Indeed, so powerful was the Norse presence that at the beginning of the twelfth century the Hebridean population was at least part Norse and the islands looked set to be a permanent Norwegian dependency. And then Somerled MacGillebrigte appeared from the mists and hills of Argyll.

Somerled—the name is said to mean 'summer sailor'—is one of the significant figures in Scottish history and with him began a colourful chapter in Hebridean life. He was the father of dynasties, the Godhead of powerful clans, yet although he is looked on as a founding figure, he seems to have been from a line that had come to the Hebrides around the seventh century, so his roots were already five centuries deep in western Scotland.

Perhaps scholars can unravel the intricacies of Somerled's past, and maybe they will dispute current theories as casually as waves toss driftwood onto a beach, but they can never remove his influence on the seaboard of the west. At some time in the past, Somerled's forebears held a Hebridean lordship, until fortune turned its back and the lands slipped into the grasp of another. Somerled's grandfather reclaimed the lands, by cunning, marriage, or the sword, yet by Somerled's time they were lost again, and the summer sailor was left with a legacy of a glorious past, but nothing tangible save the salt sting of the sea. In all probability Somerled was part Norse himself, so when he began a campaign to regain his lost patrimony it was probably not through a feeling of Scottish or Hebridean nationalism, or as an anti-Norwegian campaign. He was a man of his time attempting to carve out a place for himself in the only way he knew how; by the sword and the clinker-built ship of the Western Ocean.

Legends attach themselves to Somerled like barnacles to the keel of a galley, including his method of finding a wife. He was attracted to Ragnhild, daughter of King Olaf of Man, who controlled many of the Hebridean islands that lay beyond the seaboard of Argyll. Somerled had long admired Ragnhild, but her father had rebuffed all his attempts to court her. However the two men remained on reasonably friendly terms, so when Olaf suggested that they gather their vessels and go on a cruise together, Somerled agreed. He had an ulterior motive, for, before setting out on the expedition, Somerled bored holes in the hull of Olaf's galley, disguised his handiwork with tallow and hoped his scheme would succeed.

The two fleets sailed side by side through the western sea, their galleys surging over the long swell, oarsmen straining mightily to impress their rivals and the air filled with the call of seabirds and the aroma of sweating men. It was high summer, with the heat beating down on the ships, and gradually the tallow that filled the holes in Olaf's galley began to melt. As they approached Ardnamurchan Point the last of the tallow disappeared, and the galley began to sink. When Olaf was in danger of drowning, Somerled steered close.

'Do you need any help, Olaf?' he bellowed across the narrowing gap, as the water level in the galley rose and already some of the men were tossing their weapons overboard and preparing to swim to the distant coast.

'We're sinking.' Olaf stated the obvious. 'Can we board your ship?'

'Of course' Somerled readily agreed, 'if I can marry Ragnhild.'

Faced with a choice of marrying off his daughter to this vigorous young man or drowning, Olaf could only agree. The issue of their marriage was to have a profound influence on the history of Scotland, for the clans MacDonald, MacDougall, and MacRuaridh all look on Somerled as their ultimate progenitor.

Although relatively secure in mainland Argyll, Somerled could only glare yearningly at the scattered islands of the Inner Hebrides where Olaf's Norse still dominated. But while Somerled's kinsmen the MacHeths were waging futile war against the Crown, one of Olaf's nephews assassinated him. Olaf's son Godred the Black, recently returned from Norway, disposed of his murdering cousins, and took control of the Isles for himself. Probably used to the constant inter-family bickering of their self-stated betters, the Islesmen made no protest at these rapid changes, but when Godred began to act the despot, a man named Thorfinn harnessed their indignation and truculence into a rebellion. It seemed natural to ask assistance from Somerled, and equally natural to offer the Kingship of the Isles to Dougall, son of Somerled and Ragnhild, and grandson of King Olaf.

Thorfinn acted as his guide and mentor on a tour of the Hebrides as Dougall accepted the allegiance of the island chiefs. Those who were not immediately agreeable to yet another change of leadership were introduced to the ranked warships of Somerled and Thorfinn. Most decided that they agreed with the new lord after all.

Godred, naturally, was not amused. Gathering his own fleet, he sailed north from Man to retake the Hebrides. He was Olaf's son and heir; he had the better claim to the crown; he had right on his side, and with his galleys surging behind him, he also had the might. It was January 1156 when his longboats thrust northward through the Irish Sea, spindrift flying from their great curved prows, square sails taut with the pressure of the wind. Legend claims that Godred's vessels followed the lines and style of the Norse dragonships: long and narrow, with a shallow draught, and great flexibility. Whatever their shape, Norse ships were superb seagoing vessels, proved by centuries of voyaging and raiding from the Levant to Greenland and beyond.

It seems that Somerled's ships were different and had probably evolved to suit the waters of the Hebrides and western coast of Scotland. Termed the *naibheag* or *nyvaig*, little ship, they were smaller, probably handier, and their sternpost had a hinged rudder, a vast improvement on the old-style steering oar of the traditional longship. In the Seal of Islay, first used in 1175, there is what appears to be a fighting top on the single mast, which would be extremely useful in the hand-to-hand brawls that passed for sea battles at the time. Later representations have eight or nine ports on each side so, given two oarsmen to each oar and a further two to work the sail, one in the fighting top and the captain at the helm, each nyvaig could hold over forty men. Later Hebridean galleys carried three men at each oar so the number of men could have been higher. With each *nyvaig* possibly fifty feet long, a fleet would be an impressive sight.

Somerled had fifty-eight of these vessels under his command when he mustered to meet Godred.

Perhaps he left Dunyvaig, the fort of the little ships, in Islay, or Dunstaffnage near Oban, and headed south.

The two fleets met off the West Coast of Islay on the 6th January 1156. It is difficult to imagine the scene. A winter sea, perhaps green, with the wind flicking spindrift off curling crests and the ships rolling sickeningly as they sized each other up before locking in combat. There would be much yelling as champions on both sides shouted their defiance, and perhaps a pale sun reflected off the chain mail, spear points, and swords of heroes. Sails could be furled, men would swarm to the fighting tops, arrows could be loosed across the diminishing gap as the fleets closed, then the real madness began as Argyllmen and Hebridean clashed with the Manx and Norse. It would be a bloody, savage battle and Somerled won, forcing the Norsemen southward. Perhaps it is as well that there are no details, for all battles are terrible things, and there would be little mercy in the wild winter seas off Islay. But there was a treaty afterwards, and Somerled was left with all the islands south of Ardnamurchan, excluding Man itself, which, together with Skye and Lewis, was still held by Godred.

Now Somerled was supreme in Argyll and Lorne, and he controlled the islands from Islay to South Uist, Mull to Barra. Two years later he had to fight another sea battle off Islay to confirm his possessions, and this time the defeated Godred retreated all the way to Norway. When Godred's pleas for help to the Kings of Scotland, England, and Norway were rejected, he knew that he had lost the Isles.

With Gaelic sea power controlling the islands, Gaelic culture could reassert itself after centuries of subjugation by the Norse. Bards and sennachies reassumed their positions or assumed openly the occupations they had been forced to hide. The Church was next. Somerled asked the Celtic Church to help him revive Iona, sadly declined since its great days as the light of Western Christianity.

It may have been this appeal to a church now based mainly in Ireland that upset Malcolm, King of Scots. Unhappy at Irish influence so close to home, he countered by removing Iona's daughter foundations in Galloway and granting them to Holyrood Abbey, which deprived Iona of much-needed revenue. All Somerled could do was found Sadell Abbey in Kintyre, before concentrating on more worldly matters. To history, and perhaps to his peers, Somerled was known as Somerled, Re Innse Gall—Somerled, King of the Isles of the Foreigners, which is a resounding enough title for anybody, but unfortunately, it was not unconditionally held. The Celtic realms seem to have had a variety of degrees of kingship, and the mainland portion of Somerled's dominion was held in vassalage to Malcolm, King of Scots. The King of Norway also technically owned the islands that Somerled had won by the sword and the nyvaig. Somerled may have termed himself as King, but in a time of feudalism, he had feudal superiors. Yet, whatever the legal technicalities, he was the de facto ruler of much of the west and as long as he lived, no foreign fleet disturbed his peace.

Malcolm IV of Scots, nicknamed the Maiden, much closer to home, was a more dangerous opponent than Godred had ever been. Details of their relationship are scarce, but Somerled had fought beside his grandfather, King David in his English war of 1138 and certainly attended Malcolm's court at Perth, where his behaviour was such that he earned the nickname 'Sit-by-the-King'. Whether they were close friends or had merely formed a temporary alliance, by 1164, they were enemies, and Somerled brought a considerable fleet into the Clyde. The forces met at Renfrew, but history is confused about what happened next. Perhaps there was a battle, but one tradition claims that Malcolm bribed one of Somerled's kin to murder him. Whatever happened, the great Somerled died at or near Renfrew. Without their leader, the Hebridean fleet withdrew, and immediately the Hebrides lost their unity.

Of Somerled's five sons, two were especially

notable as they split his kingdom between them. Dougal took Lorne, Mull and Benderloch, and from him sprung the great clan MacDougall. Ranald took the style of Re Innse Gall and based himself on Islay, Kintyre and Garmoran. Ranald's son Domnall founded Clan Donald, while he was the progenitor of the MacRuaridhs. Somerled's other sons, Duncan, Alexander, and John, were poor shadows of their mighty father.

So, Somerled left a lasting legacy in Scotland, and while the sons and daughters of his clans are most renowned, perhaps he should be best remembered for one bloody January day off Islay when his fleet of little ships put the Hebrides on the nautical map of the world.

From Somerled I will jump seven centuries to one of the best clipper seamen of Queen Victoria's reign, a man whose name has nearly been forgotten by history. James Nicol Forbes.

THE CLIPPER CAPTAIN

BULLY FORBES

In an age of innovation where speed was everything, he sailed the fastest. At a time of maritime expansion, when Scotland produced a plethora of skilled seamen, he was recognised as one of the best. When iron men sailed wooden ships from one side of the world to the other, he was known as one of the hardest seamen afloat. Yet he died in poverty, and his name left a bitter taste in the mouths of maritime men.

He was James Nicol Forbes; Bully Forbes, master of *Marco Polo*, the fastest ship in the world.

Born in Aberdeen in 1821, Forbes was an eighteen-year-old youth when he arrived in Liverpool, but his evident ability soon brought him a command. Although only a brig and far from new, Forbes crossed the Atlantic to the Argentine in

PIRATES AND PICKLED HEADS

near record time and repeated the feat in case anybody thought it had been a fluke. After the first, there were other nondescript vessels, other fast voyages, and soon Forbes gained a reputation that attracted the attention of more upmarket shipping companies. James Baines, self-made man, son of a confectioner and now the owner of the Black Ball Line recognised the genius in Forbes, and soon the capable young Aberdonian was studying charts of the Antipodes.

This was the 1850s, and the Liverpool Black Ball Line was probably the most prestigious company operating between Britain and Australia, carrying emigrant passengers to Melbourne or Sydney and returning with gold. After the Hungry Forties, the Fighting Fifties opened with the glittering crystal of the Great Exhibition and broadened into the sheen of Digger's Gold as newly discovered gold fields transformed Australia from a convicts' hell to the Lucky Country where fortunes could be hacked from the harsh red soil. Specialist ships were needed to transfer such high-value cargo, and there were none better than the clipper. These were the fastest sailing ships yet developed and arguably the most beautiful ever to grace the seas. Evolved from the Baltimore privateers that gave the Royal Navy sleepless nights during the war of 1812, and the evil slavers that sped across the Atlantic with their cargoes of shame, the clippers were meant for speed. When in 1845 Alexander Hall of Aberdeen invented the 'Aberdeen bow', he gave the clippers their final raking touch. The Aberdeen bow rounded in the forward planking, so it flowed into the stem from the rail, creating a concave hull that sliced through the water. A new form of sea-racer had been born. They were delicate craft that required the sure touch of a Master Mariner and a crew of highly skilled seamen. Only the elite were good enough for the clippers, and James Nicol Forbes hoisted himself into the hierarchy with voyages that became legendary.

Baines appointed him Master, first of *Maria*, then of *Cleopatra*, both fast ships on the Australian run. With the deck of a good ship beneath his feet and twelve thousand miles of open ocean ahead, Forbes was in his element. His reputation grew with every passage, and he was recognised as possessing a rare talent. Only then did Bain offer him the ship whose name would forever be intertwined with his own. Only then did Bain offer him command of *Marco Polo*.

At first sight, *Marco Polo* was not an impressive ship, and many who knew her history shunned her as unlucky. *Marco Polo* was built on Courtney Bay, Saint John, in Canada's New Brunswick in 1850, and compared to the later Aberdeen and Clydeside vessels was no beauty. Seamen used to the grace of vessels such as *Scottish Maid* shook sad heads at her, saying that she was built like a packing case. Others said she broke her back on launching and spoke superstitiously of ill omen and death. She was 185 feet long, three-decked, and until then was the largest vessel launched in New Brunswick. Forbes, however, saw her through different eyes.

He saw her large beam that gave tremendous stability in a blow. He saw that her softwood construction made her light enough to dance over the waves rather than slog through them, despite the dour bows that gave her the appearance of a savage bulldog. Lifting his eyes to the masts, Forbes knew that they were so strong that she could carry lower and topmast stunsails even in an Atlantic gale and knew that he had found his ship. When he learned that *Marco Polo* had crossed the Atlantic with a cargo of timber and had been hawked around the coast for a full year before Paddy McGee of Liverpool had bought her cheap, Forbes smiled. He knew Paddy as a shrewd judge of a vessel. So when Baines purchased *Marco Polo* from McGee, decked her for emigrants, and married her to Forbes, it was a union blessed by the sea gods and destined to spawn the offspring of incredible passages. At just 165 tons *Marco Polo* was not huge, but Forbes guessed that she would be fast; just how fast, he would show, and the world would discover.

When the Government Emigration Company chartered *Marco Polo*, Forbes mustered the emigrants and had them separated. Single men were sent forward, single woman aft, with married couples berthed between them, amidships. With the dependable Charles MacDonald as mate, a large crew of sixty, and two doctors on board, Forbes was ready to sail.

'I'll be back in six months' he told the longshoremen of the Mersey, who laughed mockingly.

'In that tub,' they gestured to the broad-beamed Marco Polo, 'it'll take more than six months to reach Australia! If you get there at all.'

It was July 4th when *Marco Polo* slipped out of Liverpool, and on the 18th September, she arrived off Port Philip Head, just outside Melbourne. Forbes had pushed her onto a passage of sixty-eight days, which not only broke the record but beat the steamship Australia by an entire week. That was epic enough, but there was more drama ahead for James Nicol Forbes. Everybody knew that Australia was consumed by gold fever, but nobody on board *Marco Polo* was prepared for the sight of Hobson Bay.

As the main anchorage for Melbourne, Hobson Bay would normally be thrumming with activity, but that September it appeared more like a ship's graveyard. Fifty vessels lay idle, listlessly pulling at their anchors while their captains pulled at their hair in frustration. They had cargo, they had a ship, but they had no men; entire crews were deserting their craft to become diggers, and who could blame them? Life at sea was brutal, underpaid, and dangerous, with the old saying, 'the sea and the gallows refuse no man' often proving apt. Illiteracy, drunkenness, and violence were so common they were expected, so the chance of an easier life would be eagerly snatched. No doubt the crew of *Marco Polo* were equally affected, perhaps some had only signed on for the opportunity to jump ship, but James Forbes was not inclined to watch his men vanish. While other skippers used indirect methods, such as offering double wages, Forbes believed in more direct action.

Without a twist of conscience, Forbes began to accuse his crew of insubordination. He was a ship's Master, they were only foremast hands, it was his word against theirs, and the Melbourne authorities tossed the whole lot into jail. And there they remained, fretting in the heat until their captain required them for the voyage home.

On *Marco Polo*'s return trip, Forbes again tilted at a record passage. He chased the Westerlies, raced through the Roaring Forties, rounded the ferocious Cape Horn, and thrust north up the entire length of the South and North Atlantic to Liverpool. After seventy-six frantic days, *Marco Polo* sliced into Salthouse Dock in Liverpool with a broad banner stretched from foremast to mainmast. Never a man to hide his light beneath a bushel, Forbes' banner announced that *Marco Polo* was the 'Fastest Ship in the World'. Being Forbes, he did not boast that the fastest ship had £100,000 of Australian gold locked safely away. There were some who doubted that Forbes had performed the return trip in such a short time and stated openly that the ship had met foul weather and was forced back for repairs. Even James Baines could not believe that his protégé had completed the round trip.

'Sir,' a man reported to him, '*Marco Polo* is coming up the river.'

'Nonsense man,' Baines scoffed. '*Marco Polo* has not arrived out yet.'

It was less than an hour later that Baines met Forbes in person.

Many seamen were superstitious in the nineteenth century, with beliefs ranging from the idea that the soul of departed seamen lived inside the great wandering albatross, to a dislike of whistling in case it brought a storm. Forbes was no exception. Friday was reckoned as an unlucky day for seamen, but for Forbes, Sunday was his lucky day. He sailed *Marco Polo* out of Liverpool on a Sunday, passed the Cape of Good Hope on a Sunday, crossed and recrossed the Equator on a Sunday and docked on a Sunday. Possibly this plethora of holy days was a coincidence, but perhaps Forbes manoeuvred fate to his own ends.

His crew and passengers certainly bent to the iron of his will, earning Forbes the sobriquet of 'Bully'.

Legend credits him with padlocking his sheets so the crew could not take in sail. If they objected, and they might, with the decks awash with water and the high masts bending and creaking under the tremendous press of canvas, they would see Forbes at the break of the poop, watching, with a pair of revolvers in his belt. Very few people would argue with this fanatical captain, pea jacket tightly buttoned, cap jammed on his head, and long jaw dourly thrust out. The crew looked at their captain, glanced at the masts and withdrew; the sails remained in place.

On at least one occasion it was the passengers who rebelled. These old-time clipper captains always caught the constant winds of the Roaring Forties, forty degrees south latitude where the waves are mountains of grey-green death and the gales tear at a man's sanity. There was a saying of the clipper seamen that 'south of the forties there is no law, south of the Fifties there is no God', and here Forbes made his own rules. With the ship crashing through the horrendous seas the passengers appointed a spokesman to approach the captain with a request to shorten sail. Forbes did not shoot him. 'Hell or Melbourne!' he said instead, and *Marco Polo* continued to hammer along.

In the twenty-first century, speed is so much

taken for granted that it has ceased to become a virtue, but perhaps Forbes had reasons other than vanity for wanting to clip days off the record time to Australia. Nineteenth-century emigrant ships had a reputation not much better than the old slavers, with death from hunger nearly as much a threat as death from disease. Even on the shorter passage to North America, ships arrived with their emigrants in a terrible state, while *Hercules*, which sailed from Campbeltown with 380 Australian emigrants in 1852, lost 56 people, mainly from smallpox.

The return journey could be equally hazardous. Some clippers mounted a cannon aft, but most were unarmed, save for the captain's revolver, yet they carried a cargo of gold and sailed through some lonely seas. With pirates a possibility and mutiny a threat, Forbes would be well aware that a busy crew was less likely to mutiny than men who had time to grumble. And if there were pirates out there, but they would have to catch him first, and he commanded the fastest ship in the world.

The following year, 1853, Forbes was again Master of *Marco Polo*, with 648 emigrants, mostly men bound for the gold diggings. Greed for gold was pulling the hopeful, the weak, and the rootless. One passenger who did not intend to dig for his money was arrested before the ship left Liverpool, his baggage crammed with stolen jewels. Forbes mustered the remainder and gave a pre-voyage speech:

'Ladies and gentlemen, last trip I astonished the world with the sailing of this ship. This trip I intend to astonish God Almighty.'

Leaving on his lucky Sunday, 13th March, Forbes arrived in Melbourne seventy-five days later. Remaining in port a bare fortnight, he put out again in mid-June with only forty passengers but with £280,000 in gold dust, an incredible fortune in the mid-nineteenth century. Within a fortnight, *Marco Polo* overhauled the Blackwall frigate *Kent*, another gold carrier that was renowned for speed, but whose five-day lead seemed only an incentive to Forbes. *Marco Polo* arrived in Liverpool on September 13th, six months to the day after her departure. As her crew caroused in the dockside taverns, they boasted of their captain and spun tales of the icebergs they had encountered in the great South Sea.

After *Marco Polo*, Forbes took command of *Lightning*, built by Donald Mackay of Boston, probably the greatest softwood clipper builder in the world. Of Scottish ancestry, Mackay had been born in Nova Scotia but immigrated to the United States, from where his Loyalist forbears had fled. Lightning was only one of his vessels, but she was one of his best. At 244 feet, she was longer than *Marco Polo*; she cost £30,000 to build and under full plain sail had a spread of 13,000 square yards of canvas. Not satisfied, Forbes added more sails when he hoisted moonrakers above the skysails.

Still racing, still driving his ship, still with the decks awash, Forbes maintained his reputation. Seventy-seven days to Melbourne, unload the passengers, store a million pounds worth of gold dust and head back to Liverpool. Unlike other 'bully' skippers who would bellow orders from the poop and expect his mate to see them carried out, Forbes was as capable as any seaman of dashing hand over fist from the bowsprit to the foretop and aft to the spanker-boom. On *Lightning*, he had a habit of balancing on the jib boom to inspect his ship as she sliced through the seas.

If the helmsman had made a single mistake, or altered his course a fraction, James Forbes would have been tossed into the waves and churned under the keel of Lightning. That this did not happen is a testimony to the esteem in which his crew held him. Other 'bully' skippers, such as the American Bully Waterman, would never have dared give the crew that opportunity. Waterman of *Challenge* was reputed to have killed one of his crew and had to flee from a lynching mob in San Francisco. However bad Forbes' vessels were, they never approached the hell at sea of the American 'blood boats'; where seamen were worked to death or fazed until they deserted without their pay.

However, Forbes was bully enough as he stood at the break of the poop with pistols thrust prominently into his belt to prevent the crew shortening sail. But one time he went too far. However stout the spars of Lightning, they had not been designed for a seventy-five-day race across the oceans of half the world. Late in August 1854 a gale lashed out of the southwest and shattered the foretopmast stunsail boom. Freed of support, the foretopmast plunged over the side, then the foreroyal, foretopgallant, and foretopsail whipped free of their boltropes and *Lightning* was crippled. It is easy to imagine Forbes' frustration as he watched his beautiful ship disintegrate around him. For four days the clipper limped under easy sail as Forbes supervised the repairs, but he was above all a superb seaman. He understood life at sea, and Lightning, pride of Donald Mackay, skippered by the fastest seaman in the world, still sailed into the Mersey in a record sixty-four days.

That was to be the last Forbes record. Perhaps hoping to pair the fastest seaman in the world with one of the fastest ships, James Baines had ordered the Aberdeen yard of Halls to build him a clipper of 2600 tons. Halls were renowned for producing excellent, speedy small clippers, but they had no experience in vessels of this size, so they copied the design of the great Donald Mackay. Unfortunately, while Mackay built in light softwood, Halls used traditional Scottish hardwood, which was far stronger, much more durable but required a different design for speed. The £43,000 *Schomberg* was disappointingly, frustratingly, slow.

Bully Forbes had yet to discover this as he attended a banquet in his honour before he left Liverpool. He was not at his best, coming in drunk, making a speech that was only semi-coherent and saying that he would be in Hell or Melbourne just sixty-two days after sailing. Disgusted at Forbes' slurred speech and boastfulness, many guests left the room, but Forbes seemed not to care. He displayed another of his banners as *Schomberg*, 288 feet long with a triple hull, left Liverpool. 'Sixty days to Liverpool' it read, but two months later, on December 27th, she was just approaching the Bass Strait and going nowhere fast. To reach Melbourne, Forbes still had to navigate between Cape Otway and King Island, a forty-seven-mile wide passage of which the Admiralty Pilot warned:

'Approaching King Island from the westward, especially during thick or hazy weather, (vessels have) to exercise caution and sound frequently'.

Schomberg had no echo sounder, no satnav, no radar and, at that time, no captain. Thirty miles east of Otway, *Schomberg* was tacking into a headwind, with the moon casting weird shadows, and Forbes was in the saloon, steadily losing a hand of whist. Perhaps he was annoyed at the run of cards, had drunk just a little too much or was frustrated at the slowness of his latest ship, but when Mr Kean, the mate advised that *Schomberg* should go about, Forbes refused to listen. Cursing, he played another hand, and when he eventually came on deck, it was too late. The wind had dropped and *Schomberg*, caught in a westbound current, slid onto an uncharted sandbank. Forbes swore. 'Let her go to Hell,' he said, 'and tell me when she is on the beach.'

While the waves battered the clipper, Mr Kean ferried the passengers to land, but after that, it was all downhill for Forbes. Although a Court of Enquiry officially exonerated him, the Black Ball Line never again employed Bully Forbes. He became skipper of a succession of lesser ships and in 1866 left the sea forever, although there was still some vestige of the old spirit. When a duo of Americans insulted him in Hong Kong, he invited both to fight and emerged the unscathed victor. By 1867 he was a ship's watchman, and he died in 1872, to be buried in Smithdown Road Cemetery in Liverpool. His tombstone read 'Master of the Famous *Marco Polo*', which was no less than his due.

Charles MacDonald became master of *Marco Polo* but never achieved the greatness of Forbes and the ship that had once been the fastest in the world was wrecked on Cape Cavendish, Prince Edward

Island in 1883. But in his heyday, James 'Bully' Forbes had indeed astonished the world.

Other men achieved fame in different ways. One was a sealer whose name is in daily use by those people who sail to the far south, but who is virtually unknown in Scotland.

THE SOUTHERN EXPLORER

JAMES WEDDELL

How many people today have even heard of James Weddell? Very few, yet he has an entire sea named after him as he ventured where no man had gone before and relatively few since.

As late as 1820, decades after Alexander Mackenzie had crossed the Canadian Rockies when the travels of Mungo Park had opened a door into Africa, and the Great Dividing Range of Australia had been penetrated, men still doubted the existence of a continent in the far south. Perhaps this ignorance is not surprising. Of all continents, Antarctica is the best guarded. Not for nothing were the seas between forty-and fifty-degrees latitude south known as the Roaring Forties, and those between fifty and sixty degrees known as the Furious Fifties. The old nautical rhyme puts it well:

> *'South of forty there is no law*
> *South of fifty there is no God.'*

Down there in the realm of the albatross, the wind roared eternally over the surface of the water and threw an endless series of high waves at the hull and fragile spars of any foolhardy vessel. If any ship ventured further south, they would enter the region of icebergs, great floating islands of ice with the power to crush a ship or cleave its hull apart. And further south yet, amidst the fog and gales and screaming blizzards, the pack ice waited, mile after endless mile of blinding white cliffs. Only after penetrating these defences could the early mariners find Antarctica.

Such an inhospitable environment offered little to the early explorers; no treasure, no native kingdoms for trade, no land to settle, so the far south remained unknown for centuries. Occasionally a ship did touch at the fringes, but as adventurous men are attracted to the wild places of the world, these men destroyed without recording and returned without adding to humanity's knowledge of the south. Only the pursuit of wealth brought such people and the only wealth the Antarctic offered was its wildlife: whales and seals invited the hunting ships to scour the cold Southern Ocean.

It was a hard life on the sealing ships, and it

took a hardy man to command one, killing for a living among the uncharted islands and ferocious storms of the Antarctic. Few were hardier than James Weddell, Master Mariner, sealer, and explorer. History has not been kind to James Weddell, and he remains one of the least known of all Scottish explorers, yet in his own way, he was as remarkable as any. His birthplace is disputed, for although he claimed to have been born in Massachusetts, his parents were in Ostend around the time of his birth in August 1787. Weddell's father was an upholsterer from Dalserf in Lanarkshire, his mother a London Quaker and when his father died early, young James joined the Royal Navy. He was about eight years old.

Weddell was to spend the rest of his life at sea, but his first impressions of the Royal Navy were not favourable. After just one voyage under the lash of a Commander Pearse, he transferred to the merchant service, but not to a life of luxury and ease. Working mostly in the North Sea and Baltic, Weddell worked partly in colliers, crewed by some of the toughest men afloat, officered by illiterate, barefoot Geordie masters who knew every inch of the coast and who navigated by touch, sense, and instinct. At one stage Weddell was put in chains and sent aboard a Royal Navy frigate for attacking an officer, but all the time he was learning.

By the time Weddell re-entered the Navy in

1810, the Napoleonic War was in full swing and privateers rife. In 1812 a separate war began, with the young United States as the opponent, and this war gave Weddell his only sight of action. Having worked his way up from an Able-Bodied Seaman, Weddell was Master of H.M brig *Hope* in June 1813 when she captured the United States privateer *True Blooded Yankee*.

The position of Master or Master Mariner in the Royal Navy entailed responsibility for navigation, and in this job, Weddell was indeed a master. 'I think him a good seaman' stated one of his commanders, Captain Duff 'and particularly fond of Navigation, and in taking of the distance in lunar observation, I have found him unusually accurate...' Navigation was a skill that was to stand Weddell in good stead.

In August 1818, with both the French and American wars long ended, Weddell left the Navy and, after a voyage in command of *Carlotta*, was introduced to James Strachan, a partner of Strachan and Gavin of St Andrew Street, Leith. Amongst other things, Strachan and Gavin operated sealing ships and in command of one of these, the 160-ton brig *Jane*, Weddell sailed for the hazards and barely recorded coasts of the Antarctic.

Sealing tended to take place on otherwise deserted coasts, and the island groups of the Southern Ocean fitted this description exactly.

Weddell landed at the South Orkney and South Shetland group, combining sealing and surveying in a masterly display of skill. The South Orkney group had recently been discovered, or rediscovered, by the American Captain Nathaniel Palmer, but there was another group of Antarctic islands that had proved even more elusive. There had been sightings of the Aurora Islands for many years, usually in different locations, but in 1794 the captain of the Spanish vessel *Atruida* believed he had fixed their position. Weddell had resolved to settle the mystery once and for all. Basing *Jane* at the haven of St Johns on Staten Island, south of Cape Horn, Weddell sailed directly to where the Aurora Islands were meant to be 'without observing the least appearance of land.' A search of the area found nothing and 'I concluded' Weddell wrote, 'that the discoverers must have been misled by appearances.'

If Weddell had located the non-existent Auroras, they might have provided a fertile sealing ground. Instead, he had both cleared up a mystery and cleared an area of the south for safer navigation. During his surveying, Weddell named, and was the first to land on, James Island in the South Orkney group, and discovered and named the Boyd Strait in the South Shetlands. Any seaman following him would have precise knowledge of their location.

At this time there was some confusion over the

ownership of the Falkland Islands. After an erratic period where Spanish, French and British had turns at occupation, the British departed in 1774. The Spanish returned the following day but left soon after. From 1806 until 1820 there had been no official national presence, but whalers and sealers regularly called at the islands. In November 1820 Weddell anchored in Port Soledad, now Port Louis, when the frigate *Heroina*, commanded by Daniel J. Jewitt, arrived to claim the islands for the United Provinces of South America. If the United Provinces had held together, Weddell might have been witnessing history, but there was no unity in South America, the Provinces were not united, and Jewitt left the United Provinces Marine to join the Navy of Brazil. Weddell returned to Britain.

On September 17, 1822, Weddell and *Jane* sailed south again, this time accompanied by the 65-ton cutter Beaufoy commanded by Matthew Brisbane. There were thirty-five men on board the two vessels, and two years supply of food. The compasses, on which so much depended, were by Alexander's of Leith. This voyage was to be Weddell's most significant, and the drama began when Jane began to leak. Undeterred, Weddell continued and on 14th November came up with a Portuguese schooner. In a period when the Royal Navy was fighting a thankless war with the slave trade, in which Portugal played a part, it was perhaps natural for Weddell to have the schooner boarded. There were two hundred and fifty African slaves on board, and the crew of *Jane* clamoured to free them. Unfortunately, such an act would be illegal, and the schooner was allowed to proceed. Still leaking, *Jane* did likewise.

Nature compensated for the Portuguese disappointment by providing waterspouts off Penguin Island, and in the second fortnight of January 1823, Jane was among the South Orkney Islands. Again Weddell combined sealing with exploration, naming a tall hill Noble's Peak after one of his Edinburgh friends. After fixing the exact latitude of at least one of the islands, Weddell pushed further south into a surprisingly ice-free sea. Although he did not know it, Weddell was penetrating an immense bay that bit into the Antarctic continent, with the Antarctic Peninsula to the west, Coats Land to the east and high ice shelves to the south. The further south they sailed, the more the crew grumbled, so Weddell issued three wine glasses of rum to each man each day, plus over a pound of beef or pork on top of the weekly ration of flour, barley, and bread.

Further south than any other navigator had penetrated, Weddell proposed the theory that ice formed only near land and if he continued, he might sail all the way to the South Pole. Although this idea sounds strange to modern ears, the

Antarctic continent had not yet been discovered, and many scientists also believed that there was clear water around the North and South Poles.

For a while, it appeared that Weddell would justify their beliefs as, still in clear seas, he reached 74 degrees 15 minutes south. It was 20th February 1823, and Weddell was three degrees of latitude and 214 nautical miles further south than Cook had penetrated, and the furthest south in that area than any ship would reach until 1967. Although Weddell would have continued, his crew was grumbling. They were paid by the number of seals killed, not for any new discoveries they made and however fascinating exploring may have been to a shipmaster, it did not provide money to pay the bills and feed their families. Weddell pacified the grumbling men by issuing more grog and calling for three cheers, which rang ring thinly across the vast empty sea, which he named for King George IV. Not until 1900 would the name be changed to the Weddell Sea.

Discovering this sea was the peak of Weddell's career, but life at sea was never uneventful. A storm in the South Shetlands tore loose a whaleboat and froze solid the rudder. 'Never' wrote Weddell 'have I seen such an equal degree of patience and firmness as was exhibited by these seamen.' That was high praise from a Master Mariner. A sighting of a supposed mermaid at Hall Island was the last incident of an astonishing voyage, as Weddell steered for Scotland.

Returning to his home at South Hanover Street, Edinburgh, Weddell was soon back at sea, running the blockade to Buenos Aires, surviving shipwreck by clinging to a storm-lashed rock, offering the Admiralty his charts and expertise, Weddell should be bettered remembered in Scotland. Like so many mariners, he died young, but today the Weddell Sea bears his name, as does the Weddell seal, a native of this untamed area.

Weddell was only one of many Scottish explorers. Even the great Captain Cook had a Scottish father. Another who has been virtually forgotten was John Ross, who sailed to the north.

THE NORTHERN EXPLORER

CAPTAIN JOHN ROSS

The shores of the Solway in south-west Scotland have produced some excellent seamen, but none more stubborn than John Ross. The fourth son of a Wigtownshire minister, Ross was only ten when he entered the Navy in 1786 and survived three rigorous years before transferring to the merchant service. Four years later he was back in the king's service, slowly climbing the greased rungs of promotion from Midshipman to Commander.

Ross had an impressive career in the Navy. As a lieutenant in Surinam, he helped cut out a Spanish vessel that was sheltering beneath the batteries of Bilbao. As commander of *Briseis*, he faced French regulars and a prize crew when he recaptured a British merchant ship in the Baltic. In this same

Briseis, he overcame a French privateer. Wounded numerous times, captured thrice, Ross was a natural choice for anything adventurous, but by 1818 there was a severe limitation to the excitement. Waterloo had finished the French wars, the Americans were concerned with their own affairs, and the pursuit of pirates employed only a fraction of the once massive Royal Navy. However, there were still coasts to chart and mysteries to solve and, as the Royal Navy could not be kept idle, the Admiralty utilised its ships for exploration.

In this period the major nautical enigma was in Arctic waters; the search for the elusive North-West Passage, that mysterious strait between the North Atlantic and North Pacific that had baffled generations of seamen. Many famous mariners had staked both life and reputation in this mist-shrouded nightmare of ice, dead-ends, and blizzards, among them Davis, Hudson, Baffin, and Frobisher. Now it was the turn of John Ross, the minister's son. Only the previous year an experienced Arctic Mariner, the Whitby whaler William Scoresby, had penetrated as far north as 80 degrees in the Greenland Sea and found it free of ice. Taking this with other evidence, the high numbers of icebergs at lower latitudes and extreme flood levels in northern Europe, Sir Joseph Banks, President of the Royal Society, concluded that 'New sources of warmth' had appeared in the north and at his prompting the Admiralty ordered two expeditions into the Arctic. One, headed by Commander David Buchan, was ordered to sail to the Pole itself. The other, led by Ross, was to find a route to the Pacific by Baffin Bay.

Even if an explorer found such a passage, the difficulties of the route would make it unlikely to bring much in the way of new trade, the lifeblood of a commercial nation like Britain. But there might have been another consideration. With France eclipsed after the defeat of Bonaparte, Russia had emerged as Britain's main European rival. Together with her inexorable expansion across Asia towards British India, she could also threaten the security of Canada. At that time Russia owned Alaska, and her fur-trading stations were dotted along the Pacific coast as far south as San Francisco. A Naval expedition into northern waters might do no harm.

Ross sailed in the chartered whaler *Isabella* of 368 tons, accompanied by his eighteen-year-old nephew, James Clark Ross, and Lieutenant Parry in the 256-ton brig *Alexander*. There were precise instructions; Ross was to search for a current that flowed from the North or North West through the Davis Strait, the stretch of ice and sea between Greenland and North America. Then he had simply to trace the current to its source, in either the Bering Strait or the Pacific. Having negotiated the passage, Ross was to arrive at Kamchatka in Siberia and

PIRATES AND PICKLED HEADS

hand a copy of his journal to the Russian governor there, for transit to the Admiralty.

It all sounded so easy from behind a desk.

With a crew of naval bluejackets and one Inuit, John Sakehouse or Sacheuse, Ross set out. Sakehouse had stowed away to Scotland to learn to draw, speak English, and become a Christian. Now he was returning home to convert the Inuit to Christianity, on an interpreter's pay of £3 a week. Ross used the same timetable as the whalers, moving up the West Coast of Greenland in July when the ice was least formidable. It was here that the term Discovery Men was coined as the Arctic-hardened whalers scoffed at the less experienced men of the Royal Navy.

Ice began to build up as the explorers inched northward and as the first days of August passed even the reinforced beams in *Isabella* started to creak and twist. Both vessels had been strengthened for the voyage; as well as double planked bottoms, extra timber braces had been placed to support the hull, and skilful hands had reinforced the bows with iron plates. The explorers carried painted canvas roofs, which they would erect as protection against the weather should the ships be trapped in the ice. For a while it seemed more likely they would be sunk as the pressure of ice rammed *Isabella* against *Alexander*, but Ross was too good a seaman to be easily discouraged. A sudden clearing of the ice appeared to justify his optimism but as both vessels entered the dark water, a gale blew up, and the icefield closed again.

Using traditional whaler's methods, Ross attempted to carve out a dock in the ice, but his bluejackets lacked both enthusiasm and skill in the nine-foot ice saws. Luckily, the icefield passed by, and the expedition pushed slowly on, deeper into the North West as the days drifted toward the harsh Arctic winter. By this time Ross was far north of the regular whale hunting grounds so when he came across Inuit who had ever before seen a white man he was not surprised. What was astonishing was the Inuit he now met who were so isolated that they believed that they were the only people in the world. This tribe did not have the traditional Arctic skills of making kayaks or fish spears and thought the discovery ships were living creatures.

As the ships slogged on, Ross and his officers performed scientific observations and created a chart of their journey. Among their discoveries was 'red snow'—stained by vegetable matter—at the aptly named Crimson Cliffs. They also positioned Baffin Bay with more accuracy, for previous charts had it extending many miles further east. *Isabella* and *Alexander* came to Smith Sound, but a combination of thick ice and fog blocked their passage and Ross headed South West, always probing for the elusive current and a route to the west. He rediscovered a strait named Alderman Jones Sound, which William Baffin had found in the distant past, and Ross entered hopefully. There was a further disappointment when Ross saw mountains blocking his passage, so south again as fog closed on the two discovery ships.

Toward the end of August, Ross found another channel that seemed encouraging. Both ships strove westward along Lancaster Sound, with the passage gradually narrowing, snowy mountains nearby and little sign of icebergs. Fog closed again, hazing navigation, but there was no indication of the current for which they searched. Up aloft, bluejackets mustered at the mastheads, peering into the fog until, at four in the morning of the 30th August, Ross saw land ahead. There must have been terrible frustration aboard the ships as they crept on, hope dying as the fog lifted and the land ahead was revealed as a vast mountain range. Ross was confident the strait was blocked. Reluctantly, inevitably, the ships turned away.

Although he did not yet realise it, Ross had made a mistake that was to blight his career. He named the range 'Croker's Mountains' but other members of the expedition denied their existence. 'An optical illusion' said Parry and claimed that Lancaster Sound was open.

On 13th October 1818 Ross berthed at Lerwick in the Shetland Islands. He was blamed for the failure to find the North West Passage and command of the next expedition was given to Lieutenant Parry. Ross would never command another government voyage of exploration.

The whalers did not care. Quick to deride the Discovery Men, they were even quicker to capitalise on this route to new whaling grounds. Ross must have hoped that Parry would be proved wrong, but Parry's expedition sailed up Lancaster Sound and straight on, through the supposed barrier of Croker's Mountains. The strait was open, proving Ross had been mistaken. For years Ross languished in Britain, planning his return to the North, but it was to be a full decade before he sailed again to the Arctic. While Ross had been suffering semi-retirement, his nephew had been making a name for himself in three separate North Western voyages. Parry had led the expeditions, but James Clark Ross had made a bold attempt to reach the North Pole by traversing the icepack north of Spitsbergen. So when Captain John Ross proposed another voyage, it was not surprising that James Clark Ross was chosen as second in command.

Felix Booth, a gin distiller and financier, was the backer for this 1829 expedition. Ross hoped to defeat the ice by using *Victory*, a small auxiliary powered sailing ship. The theory was that *Victory's* shallow draught and steam power would enable her to go further than more traditional vessels. With enough stores to last the three years which the expedition was expected to last, £3000 of Ross's money invested and a small storeship for company, *Victory* left the Thames on May 23rd, 1829. This time John Ross was hoping to find the passage in Prince Regent Inlet.

As in the previous expedition, things did not proceed according to plan. The engines were unreliable, and before Victory passed the Lizard, she was leaking. A poor sailer, she took sixteen days to reach Port Logan in Galloway, and then the crew of the storeship refused to sail further. *Victory* left Port Logan alone. In July, Ross sighted Greenland, and soon there were icebergs nearby. Little more than a month later Ross was at the entrance to Lancaster Sound, and *Victory* eased through with no Croker's mountains appearing to block her passage. However, trouble continued to haunt them when the compass failed at the entrance to Prince Regent Inlet, but there were stars for navigation, and this crew was composed of volunteers.

Conditions were poor, with frequent fog, continued ice, and wild seas. Added to Ross's troubles, the engine was underpowered and liable to break down. There was still hope. As *Victory* inched through a landscape of desolation and vertical cliffs, James Clark Ross came into his own. Taking a sledge onto the ice, he located a safe bay for shelter. Parry had been this way before and the Rosses, anchoring between three icebergs, found the stores he had left. On 15th August, Ross sailed for Cape Garry and two days later fog, thick and cold, closed around them. They continued south down the coast of a peninsula which John Ross christened Boothia and on 26th August, James Ross, probing in his sledge, found a harbour and named it Port Logan. Still, they thrust south as the end of the month brought snow and the dread of the long winter ahead.

Six days into September and still with Boothia to the west, Ross discovered Elizabeth Harbour, but now the weather turned against them. For days *Victory* struggled against a headwind and vicious currents; only when Ross secured the ship to an iceberg was she carried clear. On the last day of the month, with 3090 miles of newly charted coastline behind him, Ross could progress no further. There was too much pack ice. *Victory* moored for the winter in Felix harbour, deep in the Canadian Arctic. There was no way Ross could have known that he was painfully heading into an enclosed bay.

After nursing the engine for so long and carrying it as excess weight on the hard passage through the summer, there must have been mixed feelings as the seamen first dismantled and then discarded the machinery. Ship and crew nestled down for the long ordeal of winter. Ross thought this a '…dull, dreary, monotonous waste.'

Less inclined to gloom, James Clark Ross proved himself one of the most adaptable of Arctic explorers. While others tied themselves to traditional methods, he learned from the Inuit. Using their techniques, he ventured from the hard-frozen *Victory* to explore the surrounding land. A five-day journey west found no passage for the ship, so he returned, to try again on the 21st April, with the same result. That month passed with no sign of the ice relenting, and in May James Clark Ross took his sledge north and west and found the western sea. Close, but impossible for *Victory* to reach. There was little consolation in discovering and naming Cape Felix.

Not until mid-September did the ice slacken; only to freeze again when *Victory* had covered a mere three miles. When spring of 1831 eventually thawed the ice, both Rosses took a small sledge team across the Boothia Peninsula. After a journey of eleven days they reached the western sea, and then parted, John Ross returned to his ship, James Clark Ross headed north to achieve the greatest success of the expedition. On the 1st June he located the magnetic North Pole and claimed it in the name of King William. Even if he succeeded in nothing else, and every mile of mapping added considerably to the geographical knowledge of one of the most complicated coastlines in the world, the world would remember James Ross for that one discovery.

For yet another winter *Victory* remained static, grasped by Canadian ice, and when the short summer eventually arrived, John Ross made the hard decision to leave his ship and strike out for the whaling fleet and safety. At the end of May, the explorers left *Victory* in a sad procession of small boats. As they reached Fury Beach, named after Parry's ship, the boats were damaged, and even the skill of the carpenter could not make them Arctic worthy. The discovery men spent their fourth winter in cabins erected on Fury Beach.

It was late summer 1833 before the Discovery men could launch the repaired boats, and Ross headed for the whaling grounds of the Davis Strait. The explorers pulled along Lancaster Sound and after mighty effort, reached Baffin Bay, but there was no sign of any whaler. Beaching their boats at the mouth of a river slightly west of Navy Board Inlet, they piled into their tents. As they slept that night, eleven days after entering Baffin Bay, the lookout glimpsed a sail. The explorers launched all three boats, but an unlucky wind carried the sail away; the disappointment must have been intense. At ten o'clock the same day another sail came into view. This whaler saw them and the mate, Hunter Etwell, thought the boats belonged to a nearby whaling ship. When they closed, Ross hailed the whaler and inquired her name; the reply was ironic

'My ship is the *Isabella* of Hull, once commanded by Captain Ross.'

Ross, gaunt and shaggy, shouted back, 'I am Captain Ross.'

'No, no,' Etwell replied, 'that won't do for me. Captain Ross has been dead these two years or more!'

This expedition restored some of Ross's reputation and gained him many honours, but he was not finished with the Arctic. In 1850, at the age of 73, he was back, commanding the 90-ton *Felix*. This time he was searching for his friend, the missing explorer John Franklin. He had no more luck with this search than he had with the North West Passage, but the attempt proves both his courage and his loyalty to an old friend. The Croker Mountains may have blighted Ross's Navy career, but they did not ruin the man.

The Northern Isles, that Ross would know well, produced some fascinating seamen, but arguably none more interesting than James Clunies-Ross, possibly the only Shetlander born in the eighteenth-century to rise to be a king.

THE ISLAND MONARCH

JAMES CLUNIES-ROSS

Scotland's maritime communities have sent seamen to rove across every sea in the world, from the high Arctic to the coast of China, but few can boast of raising a king. Shetland has that honour, for, while John Clunies-Ross was born in Weisdale Voe in the Shetland Islands on 23rd August 1786, he lived much of his life as monarch of an island thousands of miles from the grey Atlantic.

Clunies-Ross was a schoolteacher's son, but still leaned to the sea, first on coastal fishing expeditions, then, when he was just thirteen, on the deck of an Arctic whaler. In common with so many Shetlanders, he remained at sea, following the call of the next horizon. When Clunies-Ross was twenty-seven and returning homeward from a

PIRATES AND PICKLED HEADS

whaling voyage to the Southern Ocean, his ship called at the Portuguese colony of Timor in the East Indies. Perhaps the scent of the islands captivated Clunies-Ross, or maybe he just sought promotion, but he left his position of harpooner and third mate to become master of the British brig *Olivia*. Although he did not know it, Clunies-Ross had made one of those rare moves that change a life forever.

Alexander Hare, an adventurer, trader, and sometime spy, was the owner of *Olivia*, a friend of Sir Stamford Raffles who was one of the big names of the British Empire in the East. Hare, however, was not of the same calibre. He was a womaniser out for the main chance, a man who preferred to laze than to work and a man who liked to surround himself with luxury and beautiful, compliant women. As a trader in the Islands, he could work toward his dream by collecting female slaves while Clunies-Ross did the actual sailing, trading, and working.

For five years, Clunies-Ross sailed the East Indies, with the ugly task of transporting unwilling convict settlers from Java to the Banjermassin settlement on the southern coast of Borneo. European nations, including Great Britain, had a history of transporting the unwanted to settle the untamed; Border outlaws had been sent to Ulster, prisoners-of-war and petty criminals to the

Caribbean, the Americas and Australia, and now it was the turn of Borneo to experience the colonial conversion. Transporting criminals was an unpleasant job, with many convicts claiming to be innocent victims of kidnap, others guilty of only petty crimes, but Clunies-Ross had been at sea since he was thirteen. Life on board a British whaler hardened men so they could ignore the sufferings of others, even when disease killed scores of convicts, or they suffered agonies in the sweltering, overcrowded ship.

It was on these voyages that Clunies-Ross first became aware of Hare's activities as he used female slaves for sexual favours. Clunies-Ross could resist such temptations, but Hare was a man of loose morals. Shocked by Hare's behaviour, Clunies-Ross complained to the government.

At length, Clunies-Ross sailed back to London to report on the state of affairs among the Islands. However much of a Master he had been on his ship, he was only another seaman in London, and a press-gang chased him through the front door of a private house. In a scenario that could hardly be duplicated in fiction, Clunies-Ross was greeted by a beautiful young woman, the daughter of the house, fell in love and married. Her name was Elizabeth, she bore him a son, and they planned to sail back East and establish a Christian colony in the Isles.

Temporarily leaving his new family in Britain,

Clunies-Ross returned to sea, where he searched for a suitable island on which to settle. It seems that Clunies-Ross and Hare entered into a business partnership, buying spices and peppers in the Islands, storing them on an island and shipping them to Britain when there was a shortage. The island Clunies-Ross chose was one of the Cocos group, and in 1825 he decided that Cocos Islands would be a perfect place to settle. They were remote, being hundreds of miles North West of Australia, safe from pirate attacks, and with the Royal Navy supreme at sea, no other nation would dare claim them. They were also coral atolls, thick with coconut-palms and bright with seabirds and land crabs; to a man used to the storms of the Arctic regions, such a place would seem like paradise. Clunies-Ross landed on Horsburgh Island, found a tall coconut palm, and hauled up the Union Flag. All he had to do now was send for his wife and family.

Some men stumble over small obstacles, but Clunies-Ross was a man of strong character. In 1827 he brought over his family, together with his mother-in-law, Mrs Dymoke, and eight sturdy Scottish seamen who were not backward in exchanging the drizzle and chill of the North Sea for the sun of the Indian Ocean. There was only one minor fly in the paradise ointment; Alexander Hare had also settled on Horsburgh, together with a handful of male servants and forty slave women from places such as Bali, Celebes, Sumatra, and South Africa. Neither colony was pleased to see the other. Out of all the islands in the East, it was ironic that both men had chosen Horsburgh, and doubly ironic that it had been Clunies-Ross's brother who had brought Hare here.

Foolishly, Hare and his women tried to throw Clunies-Ross off Horsburgh, but the Shetlander and his men easily repulsed their attack. Hare rapidly withdrew to a nearby island. Building a high stockade in which to keep his slaves, Hare glowered at Clunies-Ross from what was soon known as Prison Island. Where force and scowls had failed, Hare attempted bribery, sending rum and pork to the Scottish seamen as they celebrated St Andrews Day. The Scots seamen already knew about the assorted female slaves; some seamen had swum the channel to visit the women, even bringing a few back.

'Stay away from my flower garden!' Hare growled.

The Scottish seamen laughed, and freed more of the slaves, as Clunies-Ross revealed his literary leanings by naming his settlement New Selma after Ossian's heaven. At that time, James Macpherson's epic poem Ossian was immensely popular, with few people doubting its authenticity as a Celtic discovery. Clunies-Ross introduced modern

PIRATES AND PICKLED HEADS

farming techniques and built substantial houses; he exploited the fruit of the coconut-palms and watched the population of his kingdom expand as his seamen married the escapee slave women. Clunies-Ross seems to have been a complex man, for, while he could transport convicts without a qualm, the stories of sexual exploitation coming from Hare's island gave him moral palpitations. Perhaps Clunies-Ross encouraged the exodus of slaves to his own island, and eventually, Hare retreated to Borneo, where he attempted to recreate his slave state.

Clunies-Ross became ruler of a growing kingdom. He relocated to Home Island, used the Bible as a guide and created a culture that was possibly more benign than the work discipline imposed in British factories. Those Malayan slaves who came to his island were free to stay or go and could roam at will, but if they broke the law, he transported them to Java. When a brace of European settlers tried to bring American whalemen to the island, Clunies-Ross sent them away, for he knew from personal experience just how wild such people could be. His Shetland background would be handy as Clunies-Ross introduced shipbuilding, creating the schooner *Harriet* in South Island in 1835. He traded in coconut and copra with Java, encouraged HM Sloop *Pelorus* to help quell more trouble by

American whalemen and ensured that the workers in Cocos had decent pay.

The standard of living in Clunies-Ross's kingdom was high, with large airy houses for the settlers and slave quarters that were superior to the cottages or tenements in which the majority of Scots lived. However, the fact that there were slaves is surely a blight on the man's memory. There was no more trouble as Clunies-Ross ruled for twenty years, dying at the age of sixty-eight. Three years later, in 1857, the British government made Cocos Islands a dominion, but the name of Clunies Ross has not been forgotten.

Few Shetlanders can claim to have been a king, but Scots seamen did not only found kingdoms. They also served in the navies of other nations, and one Solway man became a founding father of a navy that became the greatest of them all.

THE FATHER

JOHN PAUL JONES

There are specific phrases that illuminate the pages of history, bringing alive a period otherwise consigned to the pages of a book or the disc of a computer. 'Scotland Forever' is one such, supposedly bawled out by the mingled Gordon Highlanders and Scots Greys at Waterloo. 'The British are Coming,' is another, recalling the manic urgency of the American Revolutionary War as Paul Reverie galloped to raise the buckskins.

From that same war comes the equally well remembered 'I have not yet begun to fight', a pithy statement that could be used to describe the stern early years of the conflict. Reeling from defeat after defeat, the fighting men of the infant United States regrouped, retrained, and proved themselves the equal of any nation of their time. Although most of the fighting was on land, the sea was of vital importance, and it produced one of the young republic's foremost heroes, a fighting man with few equals and a sense of audacity matched only by his skill in ship to ship combat. This man was John Paul Jones, famed as the father of the United States Navy but less known in the land of his birth.

Jones was born as unadorned John Paul in 1747, son of the gardener of the Craiks of Arbigland in South West Scotland. The Craiks were merchants, with Dr James Craik being a friend of George Washington, eventually rising to organise the American Army Medical Service. As he grew up beside the Solway Firth, John Paul could have had no notion that he too would have a strong American connection.

In his early years, John Paul lived near the shore, frequently visiting the bustling port of Carsethorn. He became interested in things nautical, examining the local shipping, playing at naval warfare with his friends, and learning about the treacherous Solway Tides. At the age of thirteen, he became a seven-year apprentice to John Younger, a Whitehaven shipowner. For four years he crossed and recrossed the Atlantic, sailing to Virginia and the West Indies so when Younger became bankrupt, John Paul had enough seagoing experience to become the third mate of the slaver, *King George*.

At that time slaving carried no stigma; some

even saw it as a method of releasing the Africans from their paganism and introducing them to Christianity and civilisation. John Paul would see the trade from the sharp end, and the sickening horror of the procedure gradually affected him. After two years in *King George* and a spell as the first mate of a vessel named *Two Friends*, John Paul quit the slave trade. He sailed home from Jamaica on the brigantine *John* and, when both her Master and mate died, John Paul brought her safely to Scotland and became her new Master.

Again he navigated the Atlantic, sailing to the Caribbean, but the ship's carpenter, Mungo Maxwell, gave offence and John Paul ordered him flogged. Maxwell's later appeal to a Marine Court was rejected, but on his voyage home to Scotland, he died. When John Paul arrived in Kirkcudbright, he was accused of causing Maxwell's death and was thrown into the Tolbooth. Released when an inquiry discovered that the carpenter had died of an unrelated fever, John Paul returned to sea.

Legend says that he spent time as a smuggler in the Irish Sea and this could be the period, but more likely John Paul was engaged in more mundane trade as Master of a sailing packet between Man and Galloway. If there is truth in the smuggling tales, it certainly would not be out of character. After the Western Ocean, the Irish Sea must have seemed cramped and, as Master of *Betsy*, he returned to the Atlantic, only to encounter more trouble. The crew of *Betsy* mutinied when John Paul refused to advance them pay and at the island of Tobago they attempted to desert. Inevitably there was a confrontation, and John Paul killed the ringleader. After the affair of Maxwell, this killing changed Paul's life. He seems to have inherited Craik land in Fredericksburg, Virginia and fled there, changing his name to John Paul Jones.

Nevertheless, the change of name did not grant Jones a more comfortable life. Within a couple of years, thirteen of the American colonies had risen in rebellion, and Great Britain was threatening retribution. On the 7th December 1775, Jones was commissioned a senior lieutenant in the United States' Continental Navy and set out to make his name.

Jones had initially gone to sea to make enough money to buy his own land; now he became something of a society climber and a neat, nearly a dandified, dresser. He was also a Freemason and an experienced seaman, the type of recruit any embryo navy would be happy to employ. As First Lieutenant of *Alfred*, an ex-merchant ship now carrying thirty guns, Jones was involved in action against the Royal Navy. He must have acquitted himself well for in May 1776 he was appointed Commander of *Providence*.

Between August and October Jones took

Providence on a successful cruise against British shipping and was rewarded with the command of his old ship *Alfred*. With the British army heavily engaged in America, there was a great deal of shipping carrying munitions across the Atlantic and along the North American seaboard. John Paul Jones did not have to sail far to find an enemy, and under his command, *Alfred* became a renowned commerce raider.

When Jones began to indulge in naval politics, he was removed from his command, and for months, while rival armies marched and countermarched from Canada to the Carolinas and British shipping carried thousands of reinforcements across the Atlantic, Jones sat idle. Perhaps realising the futility of leaving an able commander on the beach, the naval hierarchy recalled Jones to duty and presented him with *Ranger*, a Boston-based 20-gun square-rigged sloop. After a worrying period, while Gentleman John Burgoyne got himself trapped at Saratoga and Jones prepared his sloop for war, *Ranger* slipped out of the harbour and headed for France. It was November 1777.

Sliding out of Brest one morning in April, with the emporium of half the world's trade as a target, Jones headed for the Irish Sea. It was an area he knew well, and he attacked two British merchant ships even before he reached Belfast Lough. The sloop HMS *Drake* was anchored in the lough and Jones dropped his anchor above hers, hoping to swing round to *Drake*'s bows so he could board. It was a brave attempt foiled only by a strong wind and when the weather worsened Jones had to seek shelter. He headed for Whitehaven harbour in Scotland and the rich pickings of some hundreds of small craft, mainly fishing boats and coasters, which sheltered there. The fickle wind eased, spoiling Jones' plan and instead of bringing *Ranger* into harbour he launched a two-pronged attack, each prong consisting of one ship's boat.

Jones intended each boat to neutralise one of the two batteries that defended Whitehaven but while the boat he commanded was successful the crew of the second vessel had found a nearby tavern and began to fraternise with their government's enemies. Such things happen in a war between cousins. More professional than his crew, Jones spiked the guns of both batteries and withdrew, burning an unlucky fishing coble by way of farewell.

In terms of major warfare, Jones attack was not even a pinprick; in terms of national prestige, it was something of a disaster. To a nation whose boast was 'Britannia rules the waves' and that considered itself something of an expert in maritime matters, any naval setback was of immense importance. And John Paul Jones had not yet finished with Britannia.

On the 23rd April 1778, he dropped anchor in Kirkcudbright Bay and attempted the even more audacious exploit of kidnapping the Earl of Selkirk. Again putting his local knowledge to use, Jones struck at the Earl's seat in St Mary's Isle but found him not at home. Where other raiding parties, including British redcoats, might have wrecked and looted indiscriminately, Jones' men contented themselves with lifting the Earl's silver. Even this minor piece of plunder weighed on Jones conscience, and he later reimbursed the Earl.

Next day *Ranger* returned to more conventional warfare when she met HMS *Drake* in a straight fight. If on paper the two vessels were equally armed, the 20-gun American against the 18-gun British sloop, the reality was a little different. Whereas *Ranger* had a confident crew of patriotic seamen with several successes under their belt, *Drake* was crewed by barely trained and possibly unwilling men with hardly enough ammunition for their unfamiliar cannon. Within an hour Jones had beaten them soundly and soon sent the captured British ship to Brest.

In July, France and Britain were officially at war, but again Jones was without a ship. It was not until August 1779 that he could put to sea as captain of the converted East Indiaman *Duc de Duras*, a vessel whose name he changed to *Bonhomme Richard*. Although a slow sailer, the ex-French East

Indiaman and 40-gun *Bonhomme Richard*—the name was taken from Benjamin Franklin's Poor Richard's Almanack—was the most powerful ship of the small squadron Jones commanded. There was *Alliance*, a French frigate with a French captain and an American crew, while three French vessels, the frigate *Pallas*, brigantine *Vengeance* and the small cutter *Cerf* completed the flotilla.

Jones had been ordered to divert attention from the usual French invasion plans. The French intended to land 50,000 troops in England, but disease and Spanish blundering ended the dream. Joined by two French privateers, Jones sailed for British waters. The flotilla split up and perhaps it was now that Jones cruised off the Hebrides. He turned up off Skye on the last day of the month in *Bon Homme Richard* and sailed into Loch Dunvegan, where the MacLeods had their castle. The chief, General MacLeod, was in North America with the army, leaving his factor in charge. Naturally perturbed when this formidable enemy warship appeared, the factor began to hide away anything of value in Dunvegan. Just when things were looking decidedly unpleasant, a funeral party crested the nearest hill, carrying the tacksman, Donald MacLeod to Kilmuir graveyard. Perhaps Jones thought that the funeral was an armed force, or maybe he had only entered the loch for shelter, but he up-anchored and sailed away, much to the relief of the people of Dunvegan.

In the middle of September Jones rendezvoused with the rest of his fleet off the Forth, where the sight of an allied French and American fleet created consternation. While the island of Inchmickery was hastily fortified and a minister from Kirkcaldy prayed for a miracle, Jones planned a siege of Leith. By the time he was ready to attack it was too late; either the prayers of the minister had been answered, or Scottish weather was its usual contrary self, for a violent storm sent the allies back from Leith and out of the Forth.

Instead of attacking his homeland, Jones headed south to cruise down the English east coast, chasing prizes and gathering information. The British were well aware of the threat posed by raiders, and a reasonably efficient convoy system was in operation. The Baltic convoy was due, 41 merchantmen protected by the heavy frigate HMS *Serapis*, Captain Pearson, and the 20-gun *Countess of Scarborough*. Pearson knew all about Jones and had ordered the convoy to sail close to shore for safety. On the evening of the 23rd September 1779 the rival squadrons met off Flamborough Head.

Although the allies outnumbered the British warships, the French seamen proved more adept at commerce raiding than actual fighting and the combat condensed into two individual ship to ship contests. While *Pallas* took on the smaller *Countess of Scarborough,* Jones in *Bonhomme Richard* engaged *Serapis* in what was to prove one of the most intense single ship actions of the war.

The vessels were nearly equal in firepower, 44 guns against 40 and Pearson was a capable commander, so *Serapis* began to pound the American into defeat. As with Drake, Jones intended to close and board, relying on the enthusiasm of his crew to overcome the pent-up frustration of the pressed and repressed British seamen. The vessels collided and *Bonhomme Richard's* accurate musketry quickly prevented Pearson from using his deck guns, but still, the British ship had the edge. Now came a request for the American to surrender, and the celebrated reply,

'I have not yet begun to fight.'

Washington could have said the same at Valley Forge, or Wellington after Quatre Bras. In each case, the result was the same and Jones continued the contest. There was still little to choose between the two ships. *Bonhomme Richard* had been reduced to a shambles, and some of her crew wished to surrender, but *Serapis* was also in trouble. Her bulwark had been blown to splinters, and at around ten in the evening a ribbon of flame licked from the British frigate into the sky. Unless something happened soon, it seemed possible that both ships, locked together in savage combat, would burn to the waterline. By incredible luck or remarkable skill, one American seaman ended the stalemate.

Perched on the yardarm of *Bonhomme Richard*, the American tossed a grenade into a pile of cartridges in *Serapis*. The resulting explosion caused terrible slaughter and, weakened in morale as well as manpower, *Serapis* lost the fight. At ten-thirty Pearson surrendered.

Jones and his Americans had won a notable victory but so hard fought that two days later *Bonhomme Richard* sank. Shifting his flag to *Serapis*, Jones took her into the Texel, where she remained until the year turned. Although the glory had gone to Jones, Pearson's stand had enabled the Baltic convoy to escape, so performing his duty. Perhaps if Jones had commanded a faster ship, he might have evaded *Serapis* and cut out some of the merchantmen, thus damaging Britain's lifeline. Instead, he created an enduring legend.

From the Texel, Jones travelled to Paris, received command of another ship, and sailed to the United States. With his fame, at its height, he was recommended to command *America*, at 70 guns the largest ship in the United States Navy, but after her launch, the republic handed the vessel to France. The frustration mounted as Jones did not receive the prize money he had surely earned and his attempt to gain promotion to Rear Admiral failed.

Disillusioned, Jones left the United States Navy and returned to Europe.

Russia was always open to hungry naval officers and from service as Rear Admiral in the Black Sea fleet, Jones was posted to the Baltic. From here things slid downhill. After being accused of rape, he left Russia, failed in an attempt to join the Swedish navy and in July 1782 he died in Paris from jaundice and pneumonia. It was a sad end to one of the United States first nautical heroes. However, his name is fondly remembered in the United States, and he is even known in Scotland. As the next war of the eighteenth century loomed up, another Scotsman clambered to fame. Overshadowed by the flare of Nelson, he is all but forgotten outside Scotland, but this giant of a man stood firm when his country needed him most. His name was Adam Duncan.

THE ADMIRAL

ADAM DUNCAN

One of the most potent of Scotland's mariners was a giant of a man who defended Britain from invasion and defeated a hostile fleet, and whose statue guards the site where he was born. This man was Adam Duncan, Viscount, and an Admiral of the Royal Navy.

At the back end of the eighteenth century, Britain was in a perilous position. Alone save for Portugal and the small states of Piedmont and Naples, Britain faced the frightening might of Revolutionary France, with her allies of Spain and the Netherlands. War had started in 1793, and by 1797 it appeared that the French had things nicely in hand. The grand old Duke of York had led a British expeditionary force to Europe, and then he led it back again, while great European nations took turns to capitulate to the reality of French aggression. The Royal Navy, dependant on a small body of professional officers a hardcore of volunteers and a mass of press-ganged seamen, was stretched to its limit.

Already the Navy had evacuated Corsica, Britain's last base in the Mediterranean east of Gibraltar. The Channel fleet was expected to both control French privateering and blockade the ports of western French. The North Sea fleet, composed of whatever odds and ends could be scraped together, had to guard convoys along the east coast and overawe the Dutch, a seagoing people not at all prone to acquiescence. Every thinking Naval officer knew how finely balanced was the line between security and invasion, but the bulk of the British population trusted their Navy. Confident in the strength of their natural maritime moat, the British allowed the Navy to take the strain as it had in so many previous wars. So it came as a shock in 1797 when the Naval seamen, Britain's bulwark, her first line of defence and the pride of her nation, mutinied.

It was not surprising really; life at sea was brutal, often monotonous, always ill-paid and usually dangerous. In the Royal Navy, there was also overcrowding and a total absence of leave for the hands. The Royal Navy was not a popular service, so to balance the lack of volunteers the

PIRATES AND PICKLED HEADS

Navy resorted to Quota Men. Each seaport was required to provide a quota of mariners for the Navy, but coastal towns thrust forward their disreputable characters, those unwanted at home and undesired by anyone else. The Navy accepted them all, and if the existing Naval seamen did not like the influx of this rabble of pickpockets, drunkards, and petty thugs, well, they were neither considered nor consulted. There was still a shortage of men, so the impress service continued to snatch homeward bound seamen and force them to serve his majesty, with the occasional hot press sweeping up any available man in coastal towns and villages. The King's ships were crewed by a mixture of the unwilling and the unrepentant and often officered by the unforgiving.

Here is a report from *Saunders News Letter* of 17th March 1803:

> *Thursday night there was a very severe press at the port of Leith. Every ship was stript of her hands, but we hear those belonging to the vessels about to sail for the whale fishery were liberated. The press gangs were the bogeymen of story and folklore and real fear for merchant seamen, but they did not always get their own way. Prospective naval seamen had a tendency to run, hide or call for help, and some ports had a reputation for violent resistance to the press. A*

major riot in Campbeltown sent the press scuttling back to their ship, but it was Leith that had possibly the most notorious reputation for resistance.

Here is another snippet from *Saunders News Letter*, this time from January 1793.

The sailors at Leith have determined to resist a press gang if such a measure should be adopted. The crews in the harbour have obtained arms which we sincerely hope they will have no occasion to employ. A watch is to be kept at the pier and another at Newhaven.

Yet in 1797 Leith and the other Forth ports provided one thousand fishermen who volunteered for the Navy 'in any naval capacity that was suitable to their position.' These men knew how harsh conditions at sea could be, but they also knew that the possibility of invasion was genuine.

To many seamen, conditions were not hard; they were intolerable. The worst thing, less justified than the years-old food, the incredible overcrowding and savage discipline, was the pay. Naval pay had not risen since the reign of Charles II, so the seamen who faced French grapeshot and cannonball and kept the seas free were paid only a quarter of the amount merchant seamen earned, and that was little enough. With their wives forced into poverty or worse while they were trapped in the King's service, naval seamen had reasonable grounds to grumble, but perhaps it was the quota men who started the mutiny.

The first outbreak occurred at Spithead and created consternation. Pay and conditions came under scrutiny, most of the demands were agreed, and things seemed to be satisfactorily resolved until a second mutiny flared at the Nore, in the very estuary of the Thames, with less justification and more malicious intent. Britain's defence was severely weakened at a time when continental armies were massing to invade, but two ships and one man kept the enemy at bay. That man was Adam Duncan.

At this time Duncan was in command of the North Sea fleet, blockading the Texel to contain the Dutch. At sea since the age of fourteen, he was now in his sixties, and his career had been useful rather than spectacular. He was already a veteran of four wars, from the Jacobite campaign of 1745/6 to this present emergency. Duncan had been wounded off Goree, he had gained £1000 prize money after the capture of Havana in the Seven Years War and had been involved in Admiral Rodney's fleet action off Cape St Vincent in 1780. In this last battle he had steered *Monarch* into the midst of the Spanish, saying 'I wish to be among them.'

Two years later Duncan was among them again, this time off Gibraltar, but then followed years of frustrating inactivity before he flew his flag as Admiral of the Blue commanding the North Sea Fleet. Duncan's ships were not of the highest quality. Most were elderly, some were converted East Indiamen or other vessels not considered suitable to take their place in the line of battle. With this ragtag fleet he had to confine the Dutch, who were fine mariners, brave fighters, and entirely at home in the shallow waters round their own country. It was while Duncan blockaded the Texel that the Spithead mutiny began, and the disaffection quickly spread. On the 26th April, the squadron at Plymouth had risen up and sent their captains ashore; by the 30th the North Sea Fleet, wind bound at Yarmouth was affected. Duncan was not pleased, but neither was he cowed.

Rather than give in to mutineers, he addressed them directly, and when he said, truthfully, that most of the initial demands, including an increase in pay, were being met, the mutiny appeared to peter out. The men seemed to trust Duncan, perhaps even liked him, and none of them attacked him personally. Maybe his height and breadth was a factor, but at a time when other crews tarred and feathered their officers, Duncan's men cheered him and promised to follow anywhere he led. Before they had the chance, the Nore outbreak was upon them. The crew of the 50-gun *Adamant* was again unstable in their loyalty, so Duncan transferred to that vessel, hoisted his Admiral's flag, and asked if anybody disputed his authority.

When one man, possibly expecting support from his colleagues, stepped forward, Duncan lifted him one-handed and dangled him over the side.

'My lads!' Duncan said as the mutineer squirmed above the cold North Sea, 'look at this fellow who dares deprive me of the command of the fleet!'

There was laughter then, but delegates from the Nore were already spreading their poison in Yarmouth and by the May 29th the North Sea Fleet was severely affected. As Duncan sailed to the Texel, his ships slipped off to join the mutineers. Only two remained loyal: the 74-gun *Venerable*, which was his flagship, and *Adamant*, which he had already cured.

'I am sorry that I have lived to see the pride of Britain disgrace the very name of it,' Duncan wrote; the pain evident in his words. With only two ships he had to blockade the entire Dutch fleet. If the Dutch escaped, they would escort the transports that waited to carry thousands of Dutch and French soldiers to invade. Britain was a naval, not a military power; her army was traditionally small compared to the frightening masses of the Continent. They were brave, and they would fight, but sheer numbers would surely count; only Duncan could stop a catastrophe.

While an invasion wind blew from the east, Duncan sat outside the Texel, watching, showing the flag, waiting. The Dutch had fifteen battleships, eight fighting frigates and anything up to seventy other craft, but Duncan had his own ingenuity and the traditions of the Royal Navy. Cruising back and forth among the shallows, he deceived the Dutch by signalling to a non-existent fleet that apparently lay just over the horizon. For a time, bluff appeared sufficient, but information came that the Dutch warships were coming out, the soldiers were boarding their transports, and Britain was in mortal danger. Positioning *Venerable* in the narrow passage between two shallows, Duncan took soundings to test the depth of water. He heard the results and glowered across to the continental coast.

'Then when they have sunk us, my flag will still fly.'

The Dutch did not sink him. The wind changed to a westerly; the Dutch failed to appear, and a squadron of Russian ships came to support Duncan until the mutiny at the Nore collapsed, and the North Sea Fleet returned to its station. In October, after eighteen weeks at sea, gale battered, and short of supplies, Admiral Duncan returned to Yarmouth Roads to refit and revictual. *Venerable* was so unseaworthy that Duncan's cabin leaked in the rain and 'when she has much motion she cracks as if she would go to pieces.'

On the 9th October, the bulk of the fleet was in Yarmouth when the lugger *Spectator* came inshore and fired her cannon, a prearranged signal that the Dutch had at last left the Texel. Having missed their chance during the mutiny, their luck had altered, and their passage out seemed clear. Lacking time to contact all his officers, Duncan left many on shore as he hurriedly readied for sea. By noon that day he had weighed anchor and was thumping across the North Sea, his clumsy seventy-four raising high clouds of spray in the choppy waves. The situation was critical, but this time the Dutch did not intend a full-blown invasion, but a raid on Ireland.

Wolfe Tone, the Irish patriot, had persuaded the French to bring an army to assist Ireland in her perpetual struggle for freedom. As happened so frequently, Ireland was in rebellion, with thousands of United Irishmen and others in arms against the occupying British; it was a situation not unlike the Scottish Jacobite rising of half a century earlier, and again the French intended exploitation. Tone planned that the Dutch fleet should defeat Duncan and embark an army of 15,000 men. The army would land near Edinburgh, march to Glasgow, and sail over to Ireland. It was a cumbersome plan at best, but if it had been attempted during the mutiny, it might have worked.

Duncan's two-ship blockade had held back the invasion long enough for disease to spread among the waiting army and for the mutiny to end. Even so, in a world that had recently seen established order overturned in both France and the United States, anything seemed possible. The Irish, of course, would welcome trained foreign help…

> 'Oh the French are on the sea
> Says the Shan Van Vocht
> And it's where they ought to be
> Says the Shan Van Vocht
> For old Ireland shall be free
> From the Shannon to the sea…'

However, Scotsmen stood as a guardian of Britain. The men of the Royal Leith Volunteers, Sea Fencibles, Leith Fencibles and Yeomanry joined the limping lawyer Walter Scott and the Royal Edinburgh Volunteer Light Dragoons, who galloped along Musselburgh beach each morning before their day's work. Between thousands of such volunteers and the invaders, sailed Adam Duncan's North Sea fleet.

Duncan's blockade had already persuaded the Dutch that invasion was hopeless; instead, the

Dutch naval committee ordered that Admiral de Winter lure the British ships onto the supposedly unknown Dutch coast where they would be destroyed on the shoals. Brought up beside the Tay, Duncan knew all about shoal water, and after months of patrolling the Dutch coast, he was well aware of the local hazards.

Admiral de Winter had entered the Dutch Navy in 1762 and rose to lieutenant before transferring to the French army. More successful as a soldier, he attained general rank and in 1795 returned to his homeland, where he was appointed Admiral. He had never commanded a single ship but was now destined to command an entire fleet. On the 8th October 1797 he hoisted anchor and set out to challenge Duncan. He had four 74-gun battleships, seven 64- or 68-gun battleships and five 44-or 56- gun ships supported by four frigates and six corvettes. It was not a first-rate fleet, as a battleship of 64-guns or less was regarded as obsolete, but Duncan also had ageing ships, and, most importantly, nobody knew if the so-recently-mutinous crews would fight.

Left to guard the Texel while Duncan took the main body of the fleet to refit, Captain Henry Trollope had two 74s and three smaller vessels. As de Winter cruised south, Trollope sent a lugger to warn Duncan while he followed the Dutch.

On the 11th October Duncan met him, learned

that the Dutch were heading north, and decided to force a fight in case they escaped into port. Every British Admiral dreamed of a full-scale confrontation with an enemy fleet; that way lay glory and prize money, rather than the tedium of blockade or convoy duty.

From the red flag of mutiny, the British seamen had exchanged the red, white, and blue of Union and were anxious to restore their reputation as Britain's guardians. Flying the signal for close action, Duncan sailed straight into battle and found the Dutch eager to fight. Duncan preferred to lead from the front. With a squadron of seven ships, he challenged the foremost Dutch, leaving Vice Admiral Onslow to attack the enemy rear. Left alone, the Dutch centre played little part in the battle. When Nelson used similar tactics at Trafalgar eight years later, they were considered innovative, but Duncan was first, and arguably faced a more formidable foe.

During his summer vigil off the Texel, Duncan had been piloted by one of the Forth volunteers, Edward Brown of Newhaven, who now stood beside him on the quarterdeck. Perhaps some of Duncan's success during the blockade was due to Brown, but the lesser ranks were seldom mentioned during this period. However, both shared the danger when *Venerable* tore into the Dutch formation. The battle was bitter, but both de Winter and Vice Admiral Reuter surrendered—the first Dutch Admiral ever to do so. Vice Admiral Onslow in *Monarch* destroyed three of the five Dutch ships that his division engaged.

'*Venerable*,' Duncan reported, 'soon got through the enemy's line and began a close action, with my division on their van, which lasted two hours and a half.' The fighting was so confused that the Scottish Captain Inglis of *Belliquex*, unable to understand the Admiral's signals, threw away his signal book and snarled, 'Damn it! Up wi' the helm and gang into the middle o' it!'

Whereas French and Spanish mariners invariably aimed high to disable their enemy's rigging, the more bloody-minded Dutch aimed low to cause casualties. There were eight hundred British killed and wounded including Captain Burgess of *Ardent*, but eleven Dutch vessels were captured, seven of them battleships. Unfortunately, they were so battered that they were only brought into port to be exhibited as trophies. All the same, Duncan received around £60,000 as his share of prize money.

The battle, named Camperdown after the Dutch village of Kamperdoen opposite where it was fought, ended the invasion threat, proved the loyalty of the Navy, and made Duncan a hero. Two years later Admiral Mitchell, acting under Duncan's supreme command, captured the remainder of the Dutch fleet after they had mutinied in their homeport. Not a shot was fired.

Ill health drove Duncan to retire to his estate at Lundie beside Dundee, but today Camperdown House, which Duncan's son Robert, built, stands proud within the splendid Camperdown Park as one of Dundee's most magnificent buildings. On the 11th October 1997, two hundred years after the battle, a statue of the Admiral was unveiled, with Dutch seamen as honoured guests of the city.

While war brought honour and wealth to seamen such as Duncan, many more had simply to endure the rigours and make a living as best they could. Often war interfered with married life, and the families of seamen were adversely affected. That was doubly so when the married couple were from different nations.

THE ALIEN

MILLIE MILLER

Scotland has always been a land of immigrants. Gaels, Norsemen, Angles, Normans, Flemings, and Irish have come to our shores to make their homes. Some have carried a sword and been less than friendly, others have been welcomed with open arms. Sometimes the position of the guests has been ambivalent.

When the French Revolutionary War ended in an uneasy treaty in 1802, Britain sighed with some relief, but few expected the peace to last. Sure enough, little over a year later the drums of war sounded again, the hot press was sweeping up mariners for the Navy and wives prepared to weep for their men, sent to fight people with which they had no real quarrel. At this time of suspicion, when any foreigner could be a spy, the Government passed an Alien Act that declared that no non-Briton was allowed to land without immediately declaring themselves to the nearest official.

For many Scots, however, foreigners were not at all hostile. Centuries of trade had created contacts that blossomed into mutual trust and genuine friendship so that even in the middle of a world war, the bonds between Scotland and Europe strengthened. The East Coast, in particular, had longstanding connections with the Netherlands, Norway and the Baltic countries, as Scotland was part of a North Sea trading network that survived wars and competing royal dynasties. Sometimes, however, politics complicated personal ties.

Such was the case in June 1806, when Robert Miller crossed over to Christiansand in southern Norway. As a merchant from Montrose, Miller had made the journey many times already, but this trip was a little bit special. As well as the cargo of timber that he was collecting, he was going to get married and bring his wife, the daughter of a Danish merchant, back to Scotland.

The ceremony was splendid, Robert and Anna made a lovely couple as they stood at the altar of Sogne Church, Robert admiring his bride so much that he had no eyes for the rose painted interior of the church. They spent a few days with Anna's family and made arrangements to return to Scotland. After hearing so much about it, Anna was excited to see her new home of Montrose, with its gable-ended houses that sounded so much like Norway, and the vast flocks of wildfowl that settled in the Common Loch every winter. She would never be lonely, for Montrose had so much trade with the Baltic that there were always ships slipping in and out of the harbour, many of which she would recognise. To make sure, she arranged that her sister would accompany her to Scotland, partly as a holiday, but more to act as a female companion. Millie, Anna's sister, was very young, still a teenager, but so excited at the prospect of travelling to Scotland that everybody laughed with her. Robert, the indulgent husband, agreed at once that Millie should come. So rather than return to Scotland with one beautiful Danish girl, he would have two; one for each arm. There could not have been a happier trio as they boarded the three-masted *Frow Geske* and readied themselves for the journey to Montrose.

Frow Geske was well known to Robert, and the master, Faral Beckman, had carried many cargoes of timber for him, but for the young women, the trip was an adventure. Anna and Millie examined every inch of the ship, from the holds to the soaring taper of the masts, and waved excitedly as *Frow Geske* put out to sea. The sisters stood on the poop, waving as Christiansand slipped slowly out of sight, and then Anna joined Robert in checking the deck cargo.

Newly married or not, she was a practical Danish woman and knew that any marriage was based on common sense and work as much as romance.

The passage from Norway to Scotland was well sailed, with the keels of thousands of vessels furrowing the sea, but at times it could be rough. The North Sea is no respecter of persons, not even of newly-weds, and that June the weather was coarse. Choppy seas thundered against the hull of *Frow Geske*, waves broke green on her prow and spattered spindrift as high as her topsails. Anna watched as Millie slowly changed from an excited teenager to a sick young girl. Rather than acting the wife, Anna became a nurse to her sister, holding her head, comforting her as *Frow Geske* heaved, tossed, and spun with every lurch of the sea. Eventually, the motion became too much even for Anna, who also succumbed to seasickness. Now it was Robert's turn to act the nurse as he cared for both the women in his life. They were not so pretty now as they retched and sweated and groaned in the ship; rather than step ashore in Montrose with two young beauties, Robert thought for a while that he would have to carry them ashore, so badly were they affected.

And the weather was not improving. Indeed, it grew worse as *Frow Geske* neared Scotland. The wind turned, blowing from the south and east so that the ship was blown toward the harsh cliffs of

Buchan. Faral Beckman called over Robert. 'We'll have to shelter!' The captain was forced to shout above the shriek of the wind in the rigging.

Only the storm sails were set now, as *Frow Geske* bucked madly in the sea, one second her bowsprit dipping toward the wave, the next pointing to the ripped grey clouds as the ship danced a crazy jig.

Thinking of his new wife and her sister suffering agonies down below, Robert was happy to agree. True his timber would be late in arriving, but that hardly mattered compared to the comfort of his wife. What a welcome to Scotland! Nodding thankfully, Beckman steered for the Bay of Fraserburgh, where there was an almost immediate difference in the motion.

When Robert clambered to the tiny cubby-hole of a cabin, his wife looked up, her face drawn, more green than white, her hair now lank and damp. 'Are we there? Have we reached Montrose?'

Millie could not speak, she lay face down on the cot, groaning softly and looking even younger than her sixteen years. Sadly, Robert had to shake his head.

'No, I'm afraid not. We've put into Fraserburgh for shelter. We've got a day or so to sail yet.' He thought of the contrary winds and the look of the sea. An experienced mariner, he knew that they might be a week or more unless the wind changed. 'Maybe longer.'

'Longer?' Anna shuddered and then tried to look brave. 'Well, it'll be worth it when we reach home.' It was when she put a comforting hand on Millie's shoulder that Robert knew he could not subject his wife to any more of this buffeting.

'No, let's not sail around. We can put ashore here and travel down by post-chaise. It's June, you can see Scotland at its best—make it into a trip.'

Beckman screwed up his face when he heard. 'It's not legal, landing like that, there might be complications,' but when he saw the pathetic faces of the two young women, he relented. 'But what harm can it do?'

The trip south through Scotland was a delight, with the countryside green and pleasant; what had been a savage storm at sea was only a boisterous breeze on land, and the two young women soon regained their confidence and their colour. They were quite happy as they rolled into the substantial stone town of Montrose, with the loch glittering blue and the fishing boats from Ferryden dotted amongst the tall Baltic traders. They saw *Frow Geske* beside the pier, but Beckman was not on board; instead, it was a tall, rather stern-faced officer of the Customs service that rasped on Robert's door the very day after they arrived.

'You are Robert Miller, merchant of Montrose?'

Robert admitted the fact.

'And you have recently married Anna, the

PIRATES AND PICKLED HEADS

daughter of a Danish merchant, and brought her to Scotland, together with another subject of the King of Denmark?'

'Yes, I have.' Robert could hear stirrings behind him as Anna rose from her bed, for it was early in the morning.

'I have then to inform you that you have committed an irregularity respecting the Alien Act, 43, of George III.' The Custom's Officer's voice was harsh and level. 'You landed with Mrs Millar and this other Danish subject on the 8th instant, without making a declaration, and without the master of the ship making a declaration, of the presence of an alien, as is required by the 6th section of the said Act. Furthermore, you landed with the said alien without having, and without seeking, written permission for the alien to land, as is required by the 7th section of the said Act.'

'What?' Robert put a protective arm around Anna, who was now beside him. 'What alien? My wife?'

The Custom's Officer sighed. 'No. On her marriage to you, your wife became a British citizen. It is the other subject of the King of Denmark who is the alien, the one who came with you. And in so landing an alien,' he continued, 'the master of the vessel *Frow Geske*,' The officer looked directly at Anna. 'In doing so, the master of *Frow Geske* has left himself open to a penalty of £50 sterling, while the said alien, the subject of the King of Denmark, may be incarcerated in gaol!'

'In gaol!' Robert stepped forward into the street. 'You'll not be putting anybody into the gaol, Mr Customs Collector!'

Anna put a small hand on Robert's sleeve. 'Robert, you can't walk outside like that. It's not decent, with other ladies maybe watching.'

Robert looked at her, realised that the tails of his night-shirt were flapping around his upper thighs and Mrs Pert was looking at him very intently from the house across the street. 'You're quite right.'

'And Robert,' Anna pulled him gently back. 'Should we not invite the gentleman inside the house? It's a cold morning for him outside, and he might want to meet this alien that we brought with us. After all,' she widened her eyes in a way that he found very appealing, 'the alien may be a spy of Bonaparte, come to cut all our throats!'

As the Customs Officer stepped inside the house, a very tired looking Millie emerged from her room. With her hair tousled and bedclothes crumpled and in disarray, she looked extremely young and very vulnerable.

'There! There, Mr Customs man!' Anna pointed to her sister, 'there's your alien! Doesn't she look dangerous? Quite the villain indeed! Obviously, a prime member of Bonaparte's army!'

The officer looked at Millie and shook his head.

PIRATES AND PICKLED HEADS

'She's only a wee lassie! Och Rab!' he thrust an elbow into Robert's side, 'you might have told me!'

'You seemed quite the official, Willie,' Robert told him, 'that I was not sure what to do. Anna, my wife, seems to have things in hand though!'

'So will you arrest my sister, Mr Customs man?' Anna stood beside Millie, who was still rubbing the sleep from her eyes.

'I don't believe that she is a danger, Mrs Miller, indeed I don't. In fact, I am sure that I can write a report to the Customhouse in Edinburgh that will clear everything up!'

That very day, the 13th June 1806, the Collector of Customs at Montrose wrote his report. He mentioned the bad weather on the crossing, the seasickness of the two young Danish women and their land journey through Scotland. His concluding paragraph ended with the words:

'We have not thought it proper to proceed to so very harsh a measure as to cause the poor stranger young lady to be incarcerated as her being irregularly landed seems to have been a matter of necessity.'

It was years before Robert and Anna explained the whole story to Millie, who remained with them until she found a fine Norwegian husband. It was said that her grandchildren laughed at the thought of their grandmother nearly ending in jail on her arrival in Scotland, rather than live the happy life which she did. And the letter that the Customs Officer wrote still survives, residing within the pages of a copybook inside Dundee Archives, mute testimony to the humanity of one official even at a time of great national danger.

Others who crossed the sea to visit the harbours on the East Coast were not welcome at all. One such was the privateer, Captain Fall.

THE PRIVATEER

CAPTAIN FALL

It was 1781, and Britain was at war. When disagreements with North American colonists escalated into a rebellion, France, Britain's eternal enemy, used the opportunity to declare war. What had started as a civil war escalated into a conflict that raged from India to the Greenland Fisheries and from the Baltic to the Caribbean. While small British armies skirmished in North American forests and on the plains of India, the sea war assumed a familiar form. British battle fleets blockaded the ports of France, while French and United States privateers harassed merchant shipping. Despite the similarities, this war had some unfamiliar aspects; it was unpopular among many people in Britain, and for once the sea war did not always go according to plan.

The unpopularity was evident; British people did not want to fight colonists of their own blood, religion, and language. Although the military and the navy did their duty, there was little desire to do more. The spiritual will to defeat a people that most Britons regarded as cousins did not exist. The lack of success at sea was less easy to explain. Perhaps Britain was merely outnumbered by her foes, or possibly there was a temporary lack of able commanders. Whatever the reason, French and United States privateers created havoc among British shipping and even small British coastal towns were vulnerable to sudden descents. The towns of Forfarshire, now Angus, were no exception.

At first, there was no surprise when the unknown cutter appeared off Arbroath, for many ships called at the busy harbour, but when she ran up the white lilies of France from her mizzen top and fired a single shot, there was consternation. In common with most Scottish towns, Arbroath was undefended, mainly because there had never been a need to erect shore batteries in the past. Now the townsfolk watched with dismay as the cutter launched a boat that sped shoreward, propelled by powerful strokes at the oars.

'Who are you? What do you want?' One of the Arbroath men shouted as the boat crossed the bar with some skill and hove to inside the harbour. She

PIRATES AND PICKLED HEADS

was packed with men, some hangdog, others armed with cutlasses and pistols, while long muskets protruded skyward.

'We are from an Aberdeen vessel' the spokesman said, 'captured by the 20-gun Dunkirk cutter *Fearnought*, which you see here commanded by Captain William Fall. You may have heard of her?'

Indeed. Captain Fall was well known. Rumour said that he was from an old Scottish shipowning family but now acted as an American privateer. *Fearnought* was equally notorious; only the previous day she had attacked Dunbar, firing three cannonballs into the town. Unlike Arbroath, Dunbar had some protection, and Provost Fall had organised a defence, Provost Fall against Captain Fall, cannon against cannon until *Fearnought* sheared off for easier prey. From Dunbar she had landed on a small island in the Forth, killed a few sheep, which made excellent fresh eating for the crew, and then sailed north, avoiding the Royal Navy in the Forth and Tay, until he arrived off Arbroath.

'Oh yes, we know about you.'

'Then you will know that Captain Fall is in earnest.' The spokesman indicated the cutter that lay offshore with her gun-ports grinning open and the ugly black snouts gaping at Arbroath.

'We ask, in the name of the King of France, that

the Mayor and chiefs of the town come on board *Fearnought*, to make some arrangement with Captain Fall.'

When Provost Greig came in person, he knew that his town could not defend itself against the privateer. His strategy was simple; talk, and talk, and continue to talk while he sent a messenger to Montrose for help. There were soldiers there, mainly to combat smugglers, but their muskets were better than nothing. 'Rally the town,' Provost Greig ordered, 'build up whatever defence we can, until the soldiers come.'

'We want the chief men of the town' the privateer's man repeated 'and we want £30,000 in hard currency. It's all in this letter.' He lifted a sealed letter high in the air. The boat came to the shore, men with muskets covering the small knot of people that had gathered to stare and the message was presented. Provost Greig opened it and quickly scanned the contents. As he had been told, it was an ultimatum, with a grim penalty clause. 'Be speedy' warned Captain Fall, 'or I shoot your town away directly and I set fire to it.' Then, disarmingly, the privateer finished 'I am, gentlemen, your servant, William Fall, Captain.'

Provost Greig called for a meeting of the magistrates and important inhabitants of Arbroath and read the letter aloud to them. As well as the Provost, Colonel Lindsay-Boysack was present,

PIRATES AND PICKLED HEADS

with Mr Fraser of Hospitalfield. Both gentlemen would look grave at the news and would cast anxious eyes at the smart little cutter that lay just offshore. The parish minister, Reverend Alexander Mackie, was more defiant, advising that they spurn the threat and dare the privateer to do his worst. While they debated, the town was roused; the cow herd hurried through the town blowing his horn as hard as he could. He usually drove all the town's cattle to pasture in the morning and brought them back at dusk, but this was more exciting work. The town drummer helped him, the rolling clatter of his drums clashing with the steady beat of the sea. The thirty-strong military garrison, more concerned with preventing smuggling than fending off privateers, would form the backbone of the defence.

'So gentlemen, we are agreed. We neither give this pirate the £30,000 he demands, nor do we agree to be his hostage.' Provost Greig closed the meeting. 'And may the Lord have mercy on this town of Arbroath.'

'And may the Good Lord have vengeance on this pirate and rebel Captain Fall!' Reverend Mackie may have said, for he was noted for his fiery defiance.

The few armed men took their positions as *Fearnought* opened her gunports again. That evening Fall opened fire, and according to tradition, he fired heated shot on Arbroath. If so, he was an unusual man, for few ships carried facilities for heating cannon balls, partly because the equipment was cumbersome, but mainly because of the risk of fire on board. Heated or not, the privateer's shot began to batter at the undefended townsfolk. When the first shots landed on Millhead Terrace, at the head of East Grimsby, Bailie James Renny led his entire family out of the line of fire. Mrs Renny, however, was not so keen to leave her house. Even as smoke jetted from the guns of the privateer, she dashed back inside her home, snatched her precious silver spoons and spared time to lift a piece of beef out of the pickling-tub. After all, privateer or not, she still had to feed her family. Her son must have followed her, for when a shot crashed into an upstairs room of the house, he tried to lift it. Finding the cannonball too hot to hold, he wrapped it in a handkerchief and proudly presented it to his mother as a souvenir.

As it was May, the evening was long, but darkness came at last, and Captain Fall ceased fire. Arbroath waited nervously, no doubt with some men on patrol in case the privateer should attempt a night raid. Others would hope that he sailed away, but the cutter was still there in the morning. The bombardment began again, as Provost Greig evacuated the women and children to Cairnie and the Den of St Vigeans. Cannonballs battered the town, smashing into houses at North Grimsby, East

Grimsby, and South Grimsby. Men groaned when the iron shot punctured the wall of Annie Harris's tavern, a favourite watering place for farmers on the Saturday market.

Fall sent another letter, threatening Arbroath with all kinds of evil, but with the women and children safe, Provost Greig was in no mood to surrender, and his reply said that 'the inhabitants were determined to defend the town to the utmost.'

He had little with which to fight, but stone houses could be rebuilt, and he would defend the town against any landing party. Hastily scribbling his defiance, he sent it to Captain Fall by the privateer's own boat. Already there were signs of retaliation. A musket ball could never penetrate the timbers of even the frailest of cutters, but a lucky shot might hit one of the crew. Tradition says that two men returned fire; one was known as the 'simple tailor', the other as 'Satan Barclay'. They sheltered behind the Knuckle Rock and harassed the privateer with musketry as the red-hot shot screamed overhead and into the town. With the soldiers and the manpower of the town, there were about 150 defenders, although most clutched pitchforks rather than muskets. There was also a cart disguised as a cannon by having a wooden pump fastened over its axle.

Fall was more of a privateer than he was a soldier; he captured an Arbroath boat and ransomed it for 50 guineas, captured another and demanded a 70-guinea ransom. Tradition says that the Master of one of these vessels told Fall that he was shooting too low, so Fall raised his sights and his fusillades hit the hill behind Arbroath. Men waited for a landing, clutching whatever weapons they could find as they ducked every time the cannons roared. After two hours the ship fell silent. Men poked their heads behind the walls that had sheltered them, wondering if the privateers were about to land. Was Arbroath to be subjected to mass pillage? One small boat came, and the Provost hurried to meet it, backed by the soldiers newly arrived from Montrose. There was a standoff, and the boat returned to *Fearnought*. Now men expected massive broadsides, but instead, they saw that the cutter was hoisting sail.

Perhaps Captain Fall had realised that he would get no loot from Arbroath, possibly he had not expected any resistance, but he sheared off, heading northward up the coast. Arbroath breathed a collective sigh of relief, but the incident had been warning enough. Shortly after, Captain Andrew Fraser, the Chief Engineer for Scotland, devised a plan for a shore battery at Arbroath. For weeks men toiled with stones and picks and shovels, and the town learned about gabions and defensive ditches, embrasures, and other technical terms of artillery fortifications. The defensive battery was erected

PIRATES AND PICKLED HEADS

near the Ballast Hill in front of the harbour, and soon six twelve-pounder cannons gaped out to sea. If any impudent rebel, or cheeky Frenchman, should threaten Arbroath again, he would get half a dozen cannon balls for his pains. No doubt some people hoped to see the battery in action, but Arbroath was not menaced again during that war, and shortly after the guns were in position, peace broke out.

Peace, however, was a rare commodity in the eighteenth century. Only ten years later, the drums of war were rolling again as a much more severe conflict engulfed half the world and privateers were again a menace on the seas off Scotland.

Most people know about the victories of the Royal Navy, nobody can deny the pageant of battle honours; Glorious First of June; Cape St. Vincent; the Nile; Camperdown, Trafalgar. Each one the story of triumph over odds, the battering thunder of broadsides and the lifting of the Union Flag over enemies of the crown. As always, though, there is another side to the story, for while the Royal Navy was invariably victorious in fleet actions and lost only a score or so small craft to the enemy between 1793 and 1814, enemy privateers captured a frighteningly high proportion of unarmed British merchantmen. In that period, French, Danish, Spanish and United States vessels snapped up an estimated 10,871

British merchant ships. Most captures were by privateers.

A privateer was basically an armed merchant ship with a government licence to plunder. They could be of any size, from a large rowing boat that put off for a short daylight cruise, to a large three-masted ship that could hold its own with a small man of war. During the long wars with France, hostile privateers haunted the coast of Scotland. Many have passed unrecorded, but sometimes their presence reached official ears, and a few laconic words by a Customs Officer marked the anxiety that they caused.

On the 28th March 1800, a man galloped south from Bervie, the hooves of his horse sending clods of mud skyward as he forced it on. Ignoring the dangers of the cliff, he dug in his spurs, only taking his eyes from the road to look seaward, as if in mortal terror. Arriving at Montrose, he clattered through the town, dismounted at the Custom House, and hammered at the door.

'I have urgent news from the Bervie Coastguard!'

The Customs Officer opened up, stepped back as the messenger nearly fell into the house and listened to his garbled explanation.

Most of the coastal community were aware that a cutter-rigged 16- or 18-gun Dunkirk French privateer was hunting off the north-east coast of

Scotland south of Aberdeen. On the 27th the cutter boarded *Hope* of Christiansand, found she was a neutral and released her. Both vessels were about two miles offshore, well within sight of the Coastguard, who had extended his spyglass to watch events.

The privateer was distinctive, with a yellow hull and a large mainsail as well as gaff topsails that pushed her through the sea faster than virtually any Scottish merchantman. On Friday 28th March she chased the Aberdeen brig *Ranger*, Captain Crane onto the beach, cut her out and captured her but a second intended prize, Captain Robinson's *Diligence* proved more troublesome. Rather than tamely run, Captain Robinson responded with musketry. It was a gesture of defiance that could hardly repel the cutter, but the sound of gunfire reached the shore and the Bervie Volunteers mustered to the beat of the drum.

'She's going to cut her out,' a man muttered. 'The privateer is going to capture the brigantine and sail her away; right under our noses too!'

'No! It's a raid!' His wife was more alarmed; she lifted up a child and held it tight as if to protect it from the threatening privateer. 'It's Captain Fall come back to burn Bervie!'

'There's the lads to stop him!' The man pointed backwards, where the brightly uniformed Bervie Volunteers now filed onto the beach.

Provost Hudson, the lieutenant in charge, led the Volunteers to the coast, where *Ranger* lay offshore, menaced by the guns of the privateer.

It is possible that the privateer could not come sufficiently close to Inverbervie to board the brig, while sending boats would expose their crews to the Volunteers' musketry. However the privateer remained close enough to menace *Diligence* while still interrupting coastal trade. As the day closed, two Aberdeen sloops with cargos of flax and a Cromarty sloop in ballast came in sight and the privateer hoisted her sails and attempted to intercept all three vessels.

Two of the sloops sailed for Bervie Bay, one detachment of Volunteers hurried to the old castle of Hallgreen and another lined the shore. The Volunteers along the shore opened fire on the privateer to prevent her launching her boats. Nobody hung back but Lieutenant Guthrie led his men with a valour that almost amounted to rashness. As musket balls rattled around her deck, the privateer retaliated by firing a broadside at the Volunteers, with a couple of balls crashing perilously close. Possibly apprehensive that the Volunteers in Hallgreen Castle had artillery, the privateer withdrew that night, with no Volunteer casualties.

It may have been the same French cutter who hovered off the mouth of the Don a few days later

PIRATES AND PICKLED HEADS

and succeeded in capturing Captain Shaw's sloop *Lady Dunbar* from Burghead with a cargo of wheat from Lossiemouth to Aberdeen. This time it was the Ross-shire Militia who took action, filing into some boats and putting out to sea to retake *Lady Dunbar*. The French prize crew immediately took to their boats and fled, with the privateer using her sweeps to escape.

The Montrose Customs Officer listened to the story, nodding quietly to encourage the messenger. The information was sketchy, probably dramatized, but still alarming. It was his duty to find out as much as he could, then to report everything to his superiors in Edinburgh. Accordingly, he rode the short distance to the harbour and interviewed the Master of the most recently arrived vessel. She was *Hope*, from Christiansand in Norway, and her Master, Sorn Engelson, added a little to his knowledge. Engelson said that he was passing Gourdon at about nine that morning when a vessel hailed him. She was a Dunkirk privateer of 16- or 18-guns, painted yellow, with gaff topsails. It was possible that the privateer would have boarded *Hope* but saw easier prey when a brigantine passed to the south. Engelson reported that the privateer was a very fast sailer.

Relieved, Engelson watched as the privateer boarded and captured the brigantine and could do little as it again approached. *Hope* was a trading ship, built as a carrier, not a racer, and the cutter was soon alongside, with armed French seamen swarming on deck. When Engelson produced the papers that proved he was neutral, the Frenchmen left and sailed away.

In his report to Edinburgh, the Customs Officer added that he did not know the name of the privateer, or her size, but he hinted that he might have followed three sloops that were headed in the direction of Stonehaven.

Such reports were frequent throughout the French wars and became more so as the war spread. In 1805, for instance, the Arbroath brigantine *Hunter*, bound for Norway was captured 'thirty leagues from the land' and her Master, Peter Stiven, was taken a prisoner to France. He did not return to Arbroath until December 1808.

For the ordinary mariner, and for the people who dwelled along the Scottish East coast, such events were the realities of the French Wars. Captures by privateers were perhaps only the small change of national history but they were of immense importance to the people involved. Major battles might fill the newspapers, Nelson and Wellington, Black Bob Craufurd and the Earl of Dundonald may have been lauded and honoured, but for all the protection they gave the ordinary mariners who sailed the North Sea, they may as well have been on the moon. Seamen from

Arbroath, Glasgow, Leith, and Greenock, along with every tiny creek along the Scottish coast were at risk every time they left the harbour, and there was always the possibility that the topsails of another Captain Fall would lift over the horizon.

It must have been an immense relief to the maritime population of Scotland when the last of the cannon smoke cleared from the torn fields of Waterloo, and there was real peace in Europe. Perhaps there was joy in Arbroath when Louis XVIII sat his not inconsiderable bulk on the French throne, but there would be jubilation when the gun battery on Ballast Hill was dismantled, and a shipyard took its place.

Of course, sometimes war came unexpectedly, with blame attached to the wrong people.

THE HARBOURMASTER

CAPTAIN EDWARD

Any history book will tell the story. A Serbian youth shot Archduke Ferdinand of Austria, the Austrian Empire declared war on Serbia, Russia, Serbia's ally, declared war on Austria, whose ally Germany, declared war on Russia, whose ally France declared war on Germany, who invaded Belgium to get at France. Britain, who had a treaty guaranteeing the independence of Belgium, declared war on Germany and the whole world was in flames. However, some of the people of Arbroath had another version of the tale.

It was August 1914, and only the cooling effects of the North Sea breezes kept the temperature down. The harbour at Arbroath was busy as the herring fleet deposited its nightly cargo of silver darlings, fisherwomen worked furiously with

PIRATES AND PICKLED HEADS

gutting knife and pickling barrel, and trading vessels slid out beyond the bar and across to Europe and the Baltic. At that time Arbroath was a major textile town that imported flax and exported linen items such as sails, and Captain Edward, the harbour master, knew to expect a barque containing flax at any hour.

Intent on their work, none of the fisherwomen looked up when the barque appeared on the horizon, her sails set, white and lovely on the sea. There were a few holidaymakers around the harbour, and they pointed knowing fingers as they speculated on the cargo that the barque was carrying. With only a slight offshore breeze, the harbour entrance was easy, and the barque ghosted in, furling sails as she eased to her berth. Her flag hung limp in the sullen heat.

As the harbour workers began to unload the cargo, Captain Edward received a telegram. Expecting news of a herring shoal sighted, or perhaps an extra shipload of flax, he opened it immediately and scanned the contents. At once he straightened in his seat and looked out of the open door. The harbour master's office was a small building set at the corner of the harbour. From here Captain Edward organised the entire workings of both the inner and outer harbour. He stared at his charge, wiped the sudden perspiration from his forehead and made a rapid decision.

Used to the bustling activity of the harbour master, only the holidaymakers watched as he marched aboard the newly arrived flax ship. 'I want to speak to the master!' Captain Edward demanded.

The master was a middle-aged man with blond hair. Knowing that all his papers were in order, he greeted Captain Edward with a pleasant smile. 'What can I do for you, Captain?'

Captain Edward produced the telegram that he had received and showed it to the shipmaster. The man's expression altered as he read.

'I have to inform you that our two nations are now at war,' Captain Edward referred to the content of the telegram, 'and that you are now under arrest. Please accompany me on shore.'

Unsure of the correct procedure to follow, the master of the German barque complied. The people of Arbroath were amazed to see the local troop of boy scouts march behind the Union Flag and with the harbour master at their head. They boarded the German barque and minutes later formed an escort for the bemused crew, who were marched straight to the railway station and onto a waiting train. It was a day later that the news of the declaration of war reached Arbroath, and one or two were a little confused at the sequence of events. When Captain Edward became a Liberal politician, he asked the question, 'who started the war?'

The answer surprised him. 'You did,' said a man who had witnessed the arrests of the crew of the barque before he knew that war was declared.

Perhaps surprisingly, not only men went to sea. There are numerous tales of women masquerading as men on ships, and as many of wives on board. However, in the nineteenth century there were only two known official female captains of a British ship. They were sisters and the best known is still remembered in her home port. Her name was Betsy Miller.

THE SEAWOMAN

CAPTAIN BETSY MILLER

What sort of woman would wish to captain a coal brig on the west coast of Scotland? Only the best sort, of course; the respectable, decent Betsy Miller. The sort of woman who, when facing death by drowning, addressed her crew:

'Lads, I'll gang below and put on a clean sark, for I wid like to be flung upon the sands kind of decent. Irvine folk are nasty, noticin' buddies.'

As well as a plethora of seamen, Scotland also produced the first female captain of a British ship to be registered with Lloyds. Betsy Miller is hardly known outside Scotland, yet she was unique, a woman who retained her femininity while commanding a collier brig and giving orders to a crew of Ayrshire seamen, who are hardly renowned for their quietness of demeanour. She was born

PIRATES AND PICKLED HEADS

around 1792, in Saltcoats on the Ayrshire coast, a town that could be so rough that the following year a body called the 'Protection Society of Saltcoats' was formed. These men charged a shilling to convoy women and nervous men past the roaring taverns and through the dark closes of the town.

While the harbour was busy, so were the three shipbuilding yards, one of which converted a wrecked Dutch warship into the brig *Clytus*, one of timber merchant William Miller's three ships. A busy man, Miller married Mary Garrett in 1790 and raised his son Hugh to take over the family business, while the three daughters were also active in the firm. Betsy was the oldest daughter, and worked in her father's office, occasionally accompanying him to sea, which was perhaps less unusual than is generally supposed. Betsy was fifteen when she first worked as ship's clerk on board *Clytus*, with the Sailing Master Mr Simonds keeping a watchful eye on her, but at sixteen she was already navigating between Saltcoats and Dublin.

In the early 1800s, Britain was at war, and French privateers could easily roam in the Irish Sea, but Betsy was probably more concerned with the daily grind of carrying general cargo, and especially coal, from port to port. Coal could be an unchancy cargo, liable to shift, occasionally able to burst into spontaneous combustion, and there was always the dust and sheer hard labour of loading and unloading. However, Betsy Miller seemed to accept the discomforts and dangers as she navigated the North Channel and the Irish Sea, sailing from the Clyde to the Irish ports of Belfast, Dublin and Cork, mixing with the crew and ensuring *Clytus* remained on course through the frequent spells of dirty weather that bedevil the West Coast.

Perhaps Betsy helped with some of the physical work, for she certainly kept the respect of the crew. It is an interesting picture, the young woman, long skirt clinging to her legs and hair plastered to her head by salt-laden water, hauling on lines at the side of tarry-palmed seamen from the Clyde. Her life was certainly different from the pampered ladies in Jane Austen's contemporary novels. When *Clytus* was carrying timber, Betsy would have helped supervise the loading, and when *Clytus* was a collier, Betsy would cough and perhaps curse with the rest. A collier seaman once said that working in such a vessel was 'sleeping in a travelling mine, sometimes in a bunk, sometimes in a hammock, but always aware of being in a world of coal.' Betsy would know well the taste and texture of coal dust between her teeth.

Knowing no other life, Betsy climbed from clerk to apprentice and then to command. She made *Clytus* her own, and her crew gave her all the respect that they accorded to any other Clydeside captain. Indeed with the perversity so often prevalent in Scotland, they might have taken a strange pride in serving under Britain's only female captain. They called her 'a hardy yin' and 'a regular brick.' Some even grudged her terms of affection 'a sonsy women, weel favoured, neither wee nor tall, and wi' as much sense o' humour as made life aboard gang pleasantly.'

Clyde coast seamen are not renowned for paying compliments, but Betsy surely had to earn her position when the fortunes of the Miller family dipped. A storm off Ardrossan claimed brother Hugh, and father William lost money so heavily that he became destitute. When he died in 1847, Betsy became the head of the family, in debt to the sum of £700 and with two younger sisters who looked to her for financial support.

Clytus was a brig, two-masted with a square mainsail and a fore and aft mizzen, but a deckhouse on her poop made her conspicuous. Betsy made the deckhouse into her private quarters, dressed as well as any woman on shore and peered out of the deckhouse to supervise her crew. 'Hoo's she daein noo, lads?'

She would be daein fine, with Betsy in command, but just in case of disaster, Betsy carried a shroud and was said to don it when the weather was fierce. She would be buried decently, whatever happened. Tradition speaks of a Clydeside custom of placing candles in the open windows of houses that faced the sea. If the wind blew out the candles, it was deemed too wild to sail for Ireland, but Betsy, fighting debt, could not afford to take time off.

'I don't wait for the carry,' she is said to have declared as she took *Clytus* into the teeth of the wind. There was a story that in one particularly nasty squall in Irvine Bay, not far from the spot where her brother had died, Betsy disregarded the shroud.

'Lads' she said, 'I'll gang below and put on a clean sark for I would like to be flung up on the sands kind of decent—Irvine folk are nasty, noticin' buddies.'

The crew nodded when Betsy retired to her deckhouse and afterwards claimed that it was Captain Betsy's change of clothes that helped them survive. Betsy Miller commanded *Clytus* for twenty-two years, and the Earl of Eglinton mentioned her while debating the 1835 Merchant Shipping Act. There were other storms, and always the sisters to support, so it may have been necessity rather than her 'romantic and adventurous spirit' that forced Betsy to sail until bad weather drove *Clytus* onto the Saltcoats sands. The brig was saved, and there were no casualties among the crew, and when Betsy learned that her cat and canary were also saved, she responded with a heartfelt, 'Thank God there's nae lives lost.'

Knowing this soft streak in her, Betsy's crew could often persuade her to issue more grog than was usual. It seems that she was an excellent man-manager, using kindness to the younger seamen but still being able to control the hard men that were necessary to sail a Clyde Coast collier brig.

When the *Times* mentioned her in 1852, the article said that 'she weathered the storms of the deep when many commanders of the other sex have been driven to pieces on the rocks.' There were legends, almost undoubtedly apocryphal that she had sailed as far afield as the West and East Indies. However, there was no doubt that Betsy was as careful with her money as any Edinburgh financier, so she cleared her father's debts and made enough money to keep the family in comfort. She bought the substantial '*Clytus* House' in Quay Street, Saltcoats and retired there in 1862, not far from the harbour from where her own *Clytus* had made so many voyages.

Hannah Miller took command, but the Board of Trade eventually decided that *Clytus* was too old to put to sea. The brig was left on the rocks beside Saltcoats North Pans, where she gradually rotted. *Clytus* House has also been demolished, but Betsy's ghost is said to still haunt the area, and she is still remembered in her home port, as is only right and proper.

While Betsy's memory remains in Saltcoats, that of the Dundee mariner, James McIntosh has created many legends, some slightly shaded. He was a Greenlandman, one of that rare breed of sailors who sailed north in the whaling ships to hunt in the Arctic seas.

THE GREENLANDMAN

JAMES MCINTOSH

By the late nineteenth century, there were only two British ports that sent whaling ships to the Arctic. One was Peterhead, the other Dundee, and of the two, Dundee retained her fleet for longer. Originally, Scottish whalers had hunted around Spitsbergen, then known as East Greenland, gradually extending their operations into the Davis Straits. They were after whalebone, as the strips of baleen that hung from the whale's upper jaw to filter plankton was known, and they were after blubber, the substance that lay beneath the whale's skin and acted as an insulator against the cold. The bone was used for many household articles but particularly for women's corsets; so whale hunting was an adjunct of the fashion industry. The blubber was boiled down into oil, which until the widespread use of petroleum was used for street, factory, and domestic lighting, but by the late nineteenth century was also used as a softener for jute before spinning. As the jute capital of the world, Dundee needed whale oil.

Today public opinion is firmly against whaling, but hunting was accepted in the nineteenth century, and Dundee was proud of her whaling fleet. Vast crowds gathered to cheer when the ships left port in spring, wives and sweethearts said a lingering farewell to their men, and there was music and dancing and tears. There was also a great deal of worry, for the wives and daughters of seamen knew very well how hazardous conditions could be in the Arctic. Many ships had been lost up there beyond Cape Farewell, and the barren coasts of Greenland and Melville Bay were dotted with the graves of men who had never come back.

In 1884 the fleet of sixteen ships sailed out; some with famous names, *Polynia*, *Aurora*, *Active*, *Esquimaux*, *Narwhal*; all steam-powered vessels, with three masts and a crew of experts, but there was also *Chieftain* commanded by Captain Gellatly. *Chieftain* was a smaller vessel than most Dundee whaling ships, a Lossiemouth-built three-masted schooner of 169 tons, and although she had been whaling since 1868, this was her first season hunting for the white or bottle-nosed whales. These small whales were native to the North Atlantic and

PIRATES AND PICKLED HEADS

yielded valuable oil. As was typical on whaling vessels, *Chieftain* had a crew composed of a mixture of experienced Greenlandmen and the first voyagers, or Green Men. Among the Greenlandmen was James McIntosh, Australian born but with Dundonian blood.

It was common practice for steam whalers to make a first voyage to Greenland or Newfoundland for seals, return to Dundee and head back to the Davis Straits for whales. With steam power, they could cross the Atlantic in fourteen days. Without a steam engine, however, *Chieftain* would make only one voyage a year, and she made for the area between Greenland and Iceland. The North Sea would invariably be choppy, so her figurehead of a Highland warrior would rise and fall, kicking up spray that would fly back to spatter the seamen who worked the ship. While the Green Men—the first voyagers—would flinch at the sight of heavy weather, James McIntosh, known to everyone as Toshie, would hardly notice.

From Dundee, *Chieftain* thrust north, no doubt calling at Kirkwall to pick up recruits, for the men of Orkney and Shetland were amongst the most skilled small-boat sailors in the world. On the First of May, the traditional initiation ceremony would be held for the Green Men. Similar to the tradition of Crossing the Equator, Neptune appeared on board and subjected the Green Men to various indignities including a rough shave with a blunt razor. Naturally, some were more severely treated than others were, for the wiser had brought a bottle of whisky to bribe their way out. Once the ceremony was finished, there would be dancing and singing while the fiddler or piper would send their bright notes to challenge the waiting ice. Perhaps some men felt a sense of foreboding then, as they looked around at the greasy menace of the sea, but others would dance their cares away. Toshie would be one of the latter, for he was not a man to give up, and besides, his wife and son were waiting for him back home. All he had to do was earn enough money to pay their bills and life would be fine.

As May wore on, *Chieftain* cruised the coasts of Greenland, hunting for the bottle-nosed whales. The system for whaling was simple; the whaling ship acted as carrier and mother ship, sending out her quota of small boats to do the actual hunting. Each boat would have a mixture of old hands and Green Men, with the most experienced in command. The boats were sturdy to resist the pressure of the ice, steered with a long oar rather than a rudder and open to the elements. On the 26th May, *Chieftain* had four boats out hunting whales when one of the fogs that the area is notorious for sprung up. The captain was in one boat and ordered them to stay together, but within minutes boats and ship could no longer see each other.

Even on land, fog can be extremely disorientating; at sea, in a small boat, with waves rising higher than the boat all around, the situation could hardly have been worse. It was common in such cases for the whaling ship to ring a bell to keep in touch, and perhaps *Chieftain* did, but even so the boats could not find her. The boats remained close together until Captain Gellatly sent one to search for *Chieftain*. The others watched their companions disappear into the cloying grey, the oars splashing softly into the sea. Six men in each boat, adrift on the chilling sea, their voices flat, distorted, brave words hiding the fear. There was no sound of *Chieftain*'s bell, nothing but the slap and suck and hiss of the sea.

While the three boats waited, the fourth pushed into the mist. Grey tendons parted as the bow slid forward, with the steersman on the long oar staring into the blankness. There was no sign of *Chieftain*, nothing but the clinging dank mist but the boat continued forward, oarsmen pulling and no doubt shouting. They did not find their ship but were picked up by a Norwegian sealer. The other boats continued to search as night fell, bringing the darkness of despair to the misery of insecurity.

There was a wind the next morning, shredding the mist and revealing nothing but grey waves rising on an empty sea as far as the men could see. Captain Gellatly called the boats closer together. There was no point in remaining here, he pointed out, so they had the choice of sailing in the direction where they had last sighted *Chieftain* or heading for the nearest land.

The men looked around at the heaving horizon. Two days ago they had been the predators, and this had been their hunting ground, now they were lost souls searching for safety; wherever that was.

'Where's the nearest land?'

'Iceland' Captain Gellatly stood up, balancing effortlessly in the heaving boat. He gestured to the north and east. 'It's about two hundred miles that way. With a following wind, we could be there in a week.'

There was no following wind. There was only work, and rain and the bitter frost that first froze the fingers of the seamen, and then ate relentlessly into their hungry bodies. The boats would hoist their lugsails, and steer to the hopeful horizon, with Toshie sitting chilled on the stern sheets with his hand clawed around the smooth wood of the long steering oar.

When the boat jerked in a sudden gust of wind, one man was knocked overboard, to fall behind, calling faintly, once, as his heavy sea boots dragged him down and down and down forever. The survivors sailed on, grimly, separated now by wind

PIRATES AND PICKLED HEADS

and weather and the fickle currents of the Greenland Sea. Captain Gellatly's boat reached land, and a Norwegian schooner rescued the crew. The next boat, commanded by the specksioneer, the chief harpooner, also reached Iceland, but fate was not so kind to Toshie's boat.

Whereas the others had a balance of experienced and Green Men, Toshie's boat held only two veterans. The others were new to the Arctic, new to survival in the ice. One by one they died, victims of exposure and despair. The first week passed, and still, Toshie steered them toward Iceland. Still he gripped the steering-oar with fingers like talons of ice, despite the thick woollen mitts that he wore; still, he sat on the stern-sheets. He had long ago lost all feeling in his legs as frostbite took hold, but he would not give up; his wife and son were waiting for him back in Dundee.

It was fourteen days before a Danish ship saw the tiny whaling boat sailing grimly to the north and east. At first, the Danes thought that it was crewed by corpses, but then they saw a flicker of movement from the man that was huddled in the stern. They hailed, and the man, white coated with ice, made a weak response, so they sent a ship's boat to investigate. Only Toshie was alive, and he was frozen solid to the seat. The Danes cut him free, hacking through the ice with axes until they could carry the Greenlandman on board. He was so severely frostbitten that they had to amputate both legs before the knee, but he lived to return to Scotland.

Like many of Dundee's seafaring population, Toshie lived in Broughty Ferry, and although he could not return to the sea, he was not content to sit idle. He was given a pair of artificial legs of teak, but they were too cumbersome for a man used to the mobility of a sailor, so he hunted for legs made of cork. There were none to be had in Dundee, but he could not afford to travel elsewhere, until a local minister, the Reverend David MacRae gave him a hand tricycle to help him travel. As he could not sail north, Toshie cycled south; all the way to London, where a journalist of the Pall Mall Gazette interviewed him and preserved some of his story. More importantly for Toshie, the paper also instigated an appeal, and soon he had his lightweight cork legs. Even then Toshie was not finished. He continued to live in Broughty Ferry and fathered another nine children. *Chieftain* continued to voyage to the Arctic until the 1890s, but Toshie never sailed on her again. With a family like that, he just did not have the time.

That is one version of the story. Another says that when Toshie was rescued, his boat had pieces of human bodies in it. A rumour spread that Toshie survived by eating the bodies of his dead shipmates. If true, he was following an ancient tradition of the sea. If false, then a brave man was being slandered. After this length of time, it is unlikely that the truth will ever be known.

Other men are not remembered at all, although they should be. Another Dundee seaman was the young John Wesley, whose name is unknown.

THE DUTIFUL

JOHN WESLEY

In the nineteenth century, disease was a significant factor in people's lives. Without the vast array of modern drugs that medical research has unearthed or created, people could fall victim to a frightening variety of diseases. Even today the names can bring a thrill of horror: cholera, typhus, typhoid, bubonic plague. Each disease could sweep across cities and countries, leaving scores of thousands dead and others mourning or in shock. What was terrible on land could be much worse at sea, where seamen were confined in a cramped forecastle, and food and hygiene were both lacking.

Until the sixteenth century, most voyages were relatively short, often barely out of sight of land, but the discovery of new continents brought new diseases, while longer voyages encouraged scurvy.

PIRATES AND PICKLED HEADS

Francis Drake lost a full half of his men in his first voyage to Central America, and he was reckoned a good Master. Anson, in 1744, lost half his men before he had rounded the Horn. By the nineteenth century, Dundee was a full participant in this new global trade network, with ships sailing to places as far afield as Greenland and Calcutta, Australia, and the West Indies. The benefits were evident, with factories and mills drawing new blood to the city, new buildings springing up and confidence that saw Dundee expand in every direction. To counterbalance the advantages, there was overcrowding and bad living conditions for some, while the seamen were no more immune from disease than were the huddled masses along the Scouringburn.

It was on 10th February 1821 that the Dundee brig *Neilson* left the Tay bound for the West Indies. At this period Dundee had quite an extensive trans-Atlantic trade, sending out manufactured cloth and bringing back sugar. The voyage to Jamaica was uneventful, with the master quite happy with progress and the mate as bad-tempered and harassed as his position could make him. For the second mate, a young man named John Wesley, this trip was something of a novelty, for he had never before seen the flying fish that skimmed across the glittering Caribbean Sea, nor smelled the exotic dampness of a tropical island.

'Your first time on a South-Spainer, lad?' The mate was elderly, with bright grey eyes in a nutmeg-brown face.

'A South –Spainer?' At first, Wesley did not understand the term, then he grinned. 'Oh—a ship that sails south of Spain. Yes, it is. I've only sailed coastal before, and one Baltic trip.'

'Well, just remember that all you are asked to do is your duty, and everything you refuse to do is mutiny. Do your duty, and you'll be just fine.'

Wesley nodded solemnly, for he was a solemn young man. 'Aye. I'll remember that.'

Neilson arrived in Jamaica on 13th April, unloaded her cargo with the minimum of fuss and set sail again, this time bound for Havana in Cuba. Wesley was learning his trade well; he was already a good seaman, but now he took lessons in navigation from the master so he could chart *Neilson*'s passage through the tricky Caribbean waters.

However, there was some unrest on board, with one of the seamen complaining he was unwell, but such things happened at sea. In the hard old days of the early nineteenth century, salt water might be poured on him, or, if he was lucky, he could be given a tot of rum. Later in the century, the Ship Captain's Medical Guide would recommend a 'Fever Mixture' of one drachm of nitrate of potash, three drachms of sweet spirits of nitre, a drachm

PIRATES AND PICKLED HEADS

and a half of spirits of chloroform, and a draught of water. Perhaps the seaman recovered, but on the 22nd May, one of the apprentices died of an unknown fever. Well aware of the consequences of a contagious illness on board, the master ordered that the boy be thrown overboard, together with his clothes and bedding. There would be a short, solemn ceremony, and the crew would watch with some misgivings as the body sunk to the depths. In the Caribbean, there might have been a swirl in the water as a shark tore at the corpse, and men might mutter a prayer that they were not taken next.

There would be relief on board when they arrived safely at Havana and rejoicing as the crew swarmed ashore to sample the pleasures of the ancient, beautiful port. But the fever had not left them at sea. It returned, so that one of the seamen sickened and, on the 27th May, died.

'There's fever on board,' the men muttered and gulped down more of the fiery rum to immunise themselves from reality. There would be fear among the carousing as the seamen made the grog-shops roar, but nobody expected that the master would be next to go. He sickened quickly, vomited profusely, and died noisily.

It's the fever again.' A young seaman shouted. 'We must stay ashore!'

'Ashore? Black's the white of my eye!' An older seaman rebuffed the cure. 'It's the Black Vomit! I've seen it before. The best place is far out at sea so it can burn itself out.'

The mate was next, rolling over in his bunk on shore on 6th June. Men looked at one another in fear and at John Wesley in expectation. 'Well youngster,' the older seaman told him, 'you're in charge now. I suppose we'll be heading back to the Tay?'

Wesley would be at a loss. Legally he was now in command of the boat, but he had neither experience nor authority, save that of his own personality. He would retire to the master's cabin, his cabin now, and consult the ship's papers to see where they were bound. When he emerged, his face was taut.

'All the men that died had been on shore. So we continue with our voyage, as the master had intended. That is our duty.'

Acting under orders from Wesley, the crew folded the clothes and bedding of the master, the mate and the seaman and placed them in three sea chests. Before he closed the chests, Wesley looked down, realising just how little these men had owned. Each man had one chest-full of possessions, ragged, work-stained clothes, a few personal trinkets, the Epitome of Navigation, a Bible. There was not much reward in this life he had chosen, only duty, and it was his duty that he would do. Locking the chests, Wesley placed them in the

PIRATES AND PICKLED HEADS

corner of the master's cabin, which he now occupied.

'Right lads. We've got a long voyage in front of us. Let's get on with it.'

Neilson left Havana with her cargo of sugar, caught the winds, and headed north and west across the Atlantic. Twice they hit rough weather, and the crew had to work and sweat aloft as the brig tossed and bucked in mad disharmony. They did not complain, for that was part of the sailor's bargain. And when Acting-Captain Wesley was not supervising the ship from the poop deck, he worked on his charts and log in the cabin, with the three sea chests a constant reminder of the mortality of men, and of his duty to his former shipmates. Every morning the crew examined each other for signs of sickness, every morning they breathed a thankful prayer that they were safe. Passing north about round Scotland, *Neilson* sailed through the Skagerrak and the Kattegat into the Baltic, a sea that Wesley knew. On the 13th August, after an event free passage, Wesley entered in his log that he had 'arrived safely at Elsiner, with the health of the crew continuing to be good'. The officials were not so happy, despite Wesley's assurances that the fever had been blown away by the North Atlantic winds.

'You will sail to Kensoc and perform Quarantine.' The stern-faced man told him.

'But it is my duty to deliver my cargo.' Wesley protested.

'And it is everybody's duty to ensure that no infectious fever is transmitted. You will sail to Kensoc and perform quarantine.'

While Wesley fretted and the crew checked each other for symptoms, *Neilson* sat for seventeen days in quarantine. After a day or two, the officials returned and ordered work to begin. Sweating in the summer heat of the Baltic, the crew landed the cargo on the quayside, case after case of sugar. The bandages that covered each packing case were unravelled and thoroughly washed, and then teams moved into *Neilson* herself. At that time, nobody understood the causes of infection, and the officials fought disease by fumigation. Foul-smelling smoke was blown through the ship, the bulkheads were washed, and whitewashed, the men were cleaned and scrubbed, the hold scoured with great wire brushes and scores of rats were killed. Only then was the cargo re-packed.

'Can I proceed now? I've got my duty to do.' Wesley saw the summer slowly slipping away; he knew that winter frost could come early in these latitudes and he wanted to unload and return back to Dundee that year. He had no desire to be ice-bound in the Baltic for months.

'We also have our duty. We'll tell you when.'

Eventually, *Neilson* was released, and Wesley

steered her for St Petersburg, where so many Scottish vessels had been before. Here Wesley unloaded the cases of sugar and shipped a cargo of flax and hemp for the linen factories of Dundee. This part of the voyage was pure routine, as *Neilson* sailed the length of the Baltic and across the North Sea to the mouth of the Tay. She arrived on 20th November. With the crew in perfect health, Wesley reported to the Customs Tidewaiter, telling him about the three sea chests that he had carried all the way from Havana.

'Why did you bring them back?' The Tidewaiter was curious.

'I thought it was my duty to give them to the families of the men.'

The Tidewaiter looked at him. 'Perhaps.'

The two men surveyed each other, the acting-master seeing yet another official who wanted to delay his duty, the Tidewaiter seeing a young man, already haunted by responsibility, but a man who had done the best he could.

'Captain Wesley,' the Tidewaiter kept his voice level and formal. 'Did you notice the effluvia within this cabin?'

Used to the assortment of stinks on board the ship, Wesley shook his head. 'Nothing out of the ordinary. Why?'

'I believe that the effluvia emanates from these three chests.'

Wesley shook his head. 'It is my duty to hand them back to the family of their owners.'

'I see. Is there much of value within the cases?'

Wesley considered. 'No. There was perhaps a total value of £5 between the three of them.'

'Not much for the master's widow in her old age. And less if the contents spread the Black Vomit through the streets of Dundee.

Wesley considered. One smell amongst so many was hardly noticed, £5 for the master's widow would scarcely compensate for the loss of her man, but the Black Vomit in Dundee was not a pleasant thought. His duty lay clear before him. He helped the Customs Officers load the three sea chests into a small boat and sat in the stern sheets as it rowed into the deep-water channel of the Tay. He watched as the chests were dropped, one by one, into the water, each chest disappearing with a swirl that seemed so small to signify the last possessions of a working man. Five pounds in value; only five times the price charged by Mr Bell, the respectable surgeon of Dundee, to inspect the ship one final time.

When the last chest had sunk into the Tay sands, the Tidewaiter gave the order to return to harbour. 'Don't look so morose Mr Wesley. You did your duty.'

Wesley nodded as he returned to *Neilson*. Whatever else happened, he had done his duty.

SECTION II
THE VESSELS

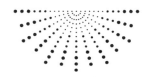

Scotland was long renowned for building elegant ships and robust ships, with 'Clyde-built' an expression that meant absolute quality. However, this section is not about the shipbuilding skills of the Scots. Far better historians than I have written long and detailed accounts of vessels built in the Clyde, the Forth, the Tay, and along the Moray Coast. This section is about some of the ships that were associated with Scotland, from the unique *Discovery* to the mystery of HMS *Hampshire* and the loss of an Arbroath fishing boat. Each story is self-contained, with no obvious link to any other, yet each highlight one particular aspect of Scotland's relationship to the sea.

The first story will be about *Discovery*, one of the most evocative vessels I have ever visited.

THE STRONG SHIP

DISCOVERY

There are many reasons for terming Dundee as a city of discovery. There were the great scientific pioneers whose research made possible X-rays, radar, and much computer technology. There are medical pioneers who worked in keyhole surgery and cancer research. There were the political pioneers, such as Britain's only Temperance MP, and the leading Women's Rights activists of their time, and there were the industrial pioneers of linen, jute, and machinery. However, many people would best associate Dundee with the lovely vessel that bears the name *Discovery*, and which lies beside the new Victoria and Albert Museum of design on Dundee's sunny Riverside.

In some ways, *Discovery* symbolises the rebirth of the image of Dundee, for, after decades of arduous service in half the oceans of the world, she returned to the city of her birth in 1986. When *Discovery* was launched in 1901, Dundee was at the height of her prestige, the Jute Capital of the world, the Whaling Capital of Britain, with hopes for a major fishing industry and with shipbuilding yards that built some of the finest vessels anywhere. The twentieth century, however, had not been kind to the city on the Tay. The jute industry had crumbled as surely as the mills and factories where it had once been spun, whaling had folded, and Dundee experienced unemployment, inadequate housing, and bad publicity. At the end of the century, things began slowly to improve. There was new and better housing, vast improvements in the town centre, new industry, a couple of vibrantly independent universities and the return of *Discovery*.

She sits proud, this wooden built, three-masted wonder, with the tall ochre funnel and the tales that cling to her as ice once clung to her rigging. The atmosphere around *Discovery* is tangible, it reeks of trips to Russia, exploration in the Antarctic and work with the Hudson's Bay Company. Yet of all her tales perhaps the most significant is one where she was not the romantic hero, but the beleaguered heroine trapped in a far-off castle and hoping to be rescued by a knight in shining armour. In this case, the knight spoke broad Dundonian, and if his armour was a Dundee built ship, his sword was highly explosive and more powerful than Excalibur.

At the end of the nineteenth century, most of the geographical questions of the Earth had been answered. Explorers such as Livingston, Clapperton, and Bruce had thrust a torch into the heart of African darkness; Stuart, Mitchell, and McKinlay had sweltered and swatted flies in the Australian outback, while Fraser, Ross, and MacKenzie had probed passages into Canada. Only Antarctica, possibly the greatest challenge of them all, was left. For centuries, man had searched for a southern continent to counterbalance the significant landmasses of the north. Australia had been a revelation, but Antarctica was still a mystery. Seamen had skirted its borders, Discovery Men such as James Ross, Weddell and Cook and the nameless sealers and whalers from New Bedford and London had landed on the bleak islands of the Southern Ocean, but still little was known. The defences of Antarctica were too deep and too formidable for the technology of the time. Nobody knew if there was indeed a southern continent, or if there was a succession of islands and mountains.

A decision was made to send an expedition south to the Antarctic. Sir Clements Markham, president of the Royal Geographical Society, was the leading promoter, while Mr Llewellyn Longstaff, a paint manufacturer and philanthropist, provided much of the financial support. Commander Robert Falcon Scott RN was chosen as leader of the expedition, and the search began for a suitable ship, one whose construction would not interfere with magnetic observations. Sparing no expense, the leaders ordered that *Discovery* be built.

Only two British yards tendered for the contract, and the Dundee Shipbuilders Company was successful. *Discovery* was one of the last three-masted wooden ships ever built in Britain, with her lines copied from the nineteenth-century Dundee steam-whalers. The new vessel was made of wood, with a complete lack of iron or steel within a 10-yard radius of the upper deck observatory, where the magnetic work would be conducted. She was 172 feet in length, 33 in the beam and weighed 1570 tons, but it was her extraordinarily stout construction that still catches the breath.

The frames of *Discovery* were of eleven-inch thick oak; they were covered on the outside by two layers of planking, together making another eleven inches of wood. Within the frames, the inner lining was four inches thick. She was built for the ice, with three tiers of beams eleven inches square running across the vessel, further strengthened by wooden bulkheads. The bows were nearly pure oak, with steel plates for even more strength. Markham called her 'the strongest ship ever launched' and it is fitting that among her company was J. Duncan, a

PIRATES AND PICKLED HEADS

Royal Naval Shipwright, from Dundee, while two of her merchant seamen were also Dundonian. On the 6th August 1901 *Discovery* slid out of Cowes in the south of England, steering for Antarctica. Her history had begun.

Discovery was bound for the Ross Sea, and although she leaked, and her masts were too short and placed too far aft, such things were expected in a new vessel. As well as Commander Scott, she had Ernest Shackleton on board, a duo of men who were to become the most famous explorers of the decade.

Not included was William Speirs Bruce, the Scottish scientist who had accompanied the Dundee Antarctic Expedition of 1892 and who was to sail *Scotia* on a purely scientific expedition to the Antarctic in 1902. Bruce's crew was composed mainly of Dundee and Peterhead whaling men, and his captain was Thomas Robertson, of Newport on Tay, known as 'Coffee Tam' because of his teetotalism. However, scientific endeavour was not as glamorous as Antarctic exploration, so while Bruce worked on painstaking research, the crowds followed the voyage of *Discovery*, southward towards the Pole.

Coaling at Cape Town, *Discovery* hit heavy weather and proved, in Scott's words 'in all respects a wonderfully good sea-boat'. She sailed past the 40th parallel, the region of the Roaring

Forties, beyond which, the old seamen claimed, there was 'no law' and further south, beyond 50, where there was 'no God'. Then they crossed the 60th parallel and hit solid ice that stopped their voyage. It was a 'grand sight' according to a Dundee seaman. *Discovery* visited Macquarie Island and sailed for New Zealand, where her rigging was refitted, and the persistent leak sought but not cured.

By the 3rd January, *Discovery* was back in the Antarctic Circle, thrusting through the ice, performing the mixed exploratory and scientific work for which she had been built. Specimens of Antarctic fauna were collected, Scott and Shackleton soared aloft in balloons to scan their surroundings, and everything seemed to be going to plan. The expedition overwintered in McMurdo Sound at Ross Island, with ice anchors not always holding *Discovery* secure from the frantic Antarctic storms and with the scientists locating over 500 different forms of life. There were long sledge journeys on the ice, an outbreak of scurvy and exploration trips even further south. There was also the realisation that *Discovery* was stuck fast in the ice.

While a relief ship named *Morning* kept contact with *Discovery* and brought some of the men home, the majority remained for a second winter in the ice. There were more sledge journeys, a diet of seals, skuas, and sheep, and temperatures that slumped so low that the thermometer shattered. However much he enjoyed the exertion of his expeditions, Scott could not fail to see that *Discovery* was in a predicament. The ice around her was seven feet thick, and there were twenty frozen miles of it between the ship and the open sea.

Arctic whalers had long known about the dangers of ice and carried great ice saws to hack out safe docks. Scott set his men to sawing out a passage to safety, but after ten days of relentless effort, the tiny result obviously did not justify the labour, so it was stopped. *Discovery*'s crew remained trapped in the Antarctic, facing a third frozen winter.

When *Morning* returned to Britain, she reported the predicament of *Discovery* to the leaders of the National Antarctic Expedition. Lack of finances forced an appeal to the government, and the Admiralty had formed a relief Committee. Scott was also ordered to return to Britain without his ship, as there was not enough money remaining for another winter in the Antarctic; however, the expedition had grown attached to *Discovery*.

The Admiralty sent two ships to relieve Scott. One was the faithful *Morning*, which had been the Norwegian whaler, *Morgen*. Built by Svend Foyn, who had done much to modernise Norwegian whaling, *Morgen* was wooden, very strong, 140 feet long and was refitted at Blackwall. The second vessel was another Dundee vessel that was to become famous throughout the world. Alexander Stephens and Sons had built *Terra Nova* in 1884. She was 187 feet long, two decked, three-masted, barque-rigged and boasted a figurehead of a demi-woman. To the old sailing seamen, figureheads were necessary, and the legend was that a bare-breasted woman had the power to calm stormy seas. Now the female figurehead of *Terra Nova* was to lead her ship south on a relief expedition for her Dundee sister. Her skipper was Captain Harry McKay, a stocky, moustached, and veteran Dundee whaling man, and her officers were pure Dundonian.

After being fitted out, *Terra Nova* sailed south. She was towed through the Suez Canal, a Scottish Arctic whaler using a French engineered canal to pass through an Egyptian desert and teamed up with *Morning* at Tasmania. Captain MacKay spent Christmas on *Morning*, telling *Terra Nova*'s Second Mate that he would be back before dark. He must have had his tongue firmly in his cheek at the time, for in those high southern latitudes there was no darkness until late February. By the 5th January, the rescue ships had located *Discovery* and they sledged fresh provisions and welcome mail across the ice.

Still reluctant to abandon his ship, Scott reported on the failure of the sawing parties but

PIRATES AND PICKLED HEADS

said that all the scientific equipment should be transferred to *Terra Nova*. Where saws had failed, explosives might work, and men set to work boring holes in the now eight-foot thick ice. It was the 15th January when probably the first explosion ever heard in the Antarctic sent shards of ice flying, and the men worked on, tired, cold, and smoke stained. They raced against time, for Scott had a fixed date beyond which he was not permitted to remain with *Discovery*. He was a naval officer, under orders, and however hard it would be, he must abandon his ship to the ice.

Slowly the twenty frozen miles shrunk, but as they did, the deadline approached. The 13th February lived up to its reputation as a bad day, with two miles of ice remaining between *Discovery* and open water, but the 14th offered more promise. As the wind howled from the East-Northeast, the men set to work. Before the morning was done, they had cleared a third of a mile, and in the afternoon, they had thinned the worst of the remaining ice. By midnight there was a passage, and *Terra Nova* nosed in, her powerful engines and stout stem pushing aside the drifting ice. Within two more days, *Discovery* was free, and the combined companies of both ships cheered as the way home was open.

There is a photograph of this event, with *Morning* and *Terra Nova* afloat in a narrow passage of ice while *Discovery* is still surrounded by a solid white sheet. The figures of men, small, black, seemingly insignificant, scurry about the ice, while white-streaked, gaunt hills rise in the background. The photograph reveals the bleakness of their situation, but also the endurance of the men and something of the haunting beauty of the Antarctic that enticed men like Scott and Shackleton to return again and again. It is a haunting scene, strangely sad, as if of a way of life and a type of man that will possibly never be seen again. It is good to know that Scotland played a full share in these times, and in *Discovery*, Dundee retains a very physical memory.

To Scott, Shackleton, and MacKay, *Discovery* was a problem rather than a memory. Even though she was free of the ice, the voyage home was not simple. On the 17th February, a gale blew up, *Discovery* grounded on a shoal, and the wind and weather smashed her sickeningly. Not until the current changed could she be worked free, to make her way north, with Scott comparing the rolling of his vessel with the steadier progress of the whaler *Terra Nova*.

While all the attention and all the kudos was directed at the National Antarctic Expedition, Bruce's Scottish National Antarctic Expedition had been equally busy. His ship *Scotia* had also been trapped in the ice but rather than plead for help,

PIRATES AND PICKLED HEADS

had managed to free herself and his scientists had carried out thorough investigations. *Scotia* took 75 deep soundings in the South Atlantic, the Weddell, and Biscoe seas, and another five hundred around the South Orkney Islands. She voyaged over 33,000 miles, surveyed 4000 miles of coastline, and made numerous observations of bird and animal life. Bruce's subsequent book, Polar Exploration, was full of valuable information and on her return to Scotland, *Scotia* was cheered by massed crowds and received a congratulatory telegram from the King.

While *Discovery* is, rightfully, preserved in Dundee, the other vessels were not so fortunate. *Terra Nova* remained a Dundee whaler, later working off Newfoundland until she was torpedoed in 1943. Scotia also became a whaler, and in 1913 she became was the first vessel on the North Atlantic Ice Patrol, instituted after the disaster of *Titanic*. She was lost when she caught fire in the Bristol Channel in 1916. *Morning*, together with the Dundee whaler *Active*, was sunk in a North Atlantic gale in December 1915.

Dundee's interest in the Antarctic did not end with the return of *Discovery*. Sir James Caird, a Dundee jute baron, financed Shackleton's Imperial Trans-Antarctic Expedition in 1913 so it could be said that the last great heroic age of exploration was primarily a Scottish and Dundee operation, with

Bruce, Scott, and Shackleton all having secure Dundee connections.

The next story is about a ship, a man, and a mystery that may not be a mystery at all, but only a fabrication derived from a few half-understood facts. I am sure somebody, somewhere knows the truth. I just have not met him, or her, or read their explanation.

THE MYSTERY SHIP

HMS HAMPSHIRE

Square and uncompromising on Marwick Head on the west coast of Mainland Orkney, the Kitchener Memorial Tower glares across the bitter sea. Not far offshore, a German submarine or mine sunk H.M.S. *Hampshire*. It may seem strange to link Kitchener with Orkney, when a mention of the name more usually brings images of the dry sands around Khartoum, or of that most famous of all posters, with the steel eyes and pointing finger: 'Your Country Needs You', yet it was in these cold northern seas that Lord Kitchener died.

There are guillemots here, and gulls, wheeling and calling and diving, and the magnificent 300 feet high cliffs with the eternal wind rasping and buffeting around the stone monument. It can be a bleak place in winter, but fitting for a military man, for Kitchener was noted for his sternness, although there was no deliberate cruelty in him. In his day, at the end of the nineteenth and beginning of the twentieth centuries, Kitchener was something of a cult figure. He was the man who avenged General Gordon in the Sudan, who defeated the Mahdi, and Kipling's famous Fuzzy Wuzzies.

It was the summer of 1916 and Britain had been at war for nearly two years. A new type of war, with six of the largest empires that the world had ever known locked in an ugly stalemate. On the Allied side, the Empires of Great Britain, France, and Russia faced the Central Powers of Germany, Austria-Hungary, and Turkey, and while the Royal Navy contested the sea with the German Imperial Navy, it was the land war that took most of the headlines.

Tsar Nicholas of Russia had invited Lord Kitchener, Britain's Minister of War, to Petrograd for talks about the situation on the Eastern Front, where the Germans threatened to force Russia out of the war. Travelling from London to Thurso, Kitchener hitched a ride on a destroyer to Orkney, the home base of the fleet. After a brief meeting with Admiral Jellicoe, Kitchener then boarded the 10,850-ton, Devonshire class armoured cruiser HMS *Hampshire*. At 16.40, on Monday 5th June 1916 *Hampshire*, with her crew of around 650 men as well as Kitchener's staff, hauled her anchor from Scapa

Flow, heading for Archangel but sailing straight into a force nine gale. She did not travel alone, for the destroyers HMS *Unity* and HMS *Victor* escorted her until the severe weather forced them back at around 18.30 in the evening. *Hampshire* continued alone, battering through the ugly green waves at over 13 knots.

The original plan had been for *Hampshire* to take an easterly passage north, but the weather forced her to the west, closer to the Orkney coast. Although the Navy did not regularly sweep this route for mines, it was believed to be safe, so close to the great naval base of Scapa Floe. However, German submarine commanders were noted for their daring and on the 28 May, Lieutenant Commander Kurt Beitzen's U-75 had laid a quota of mines. Some people claimed that the Navy was quite aware that U-75 had laid these mines, but through some failure of Naval Intelligence, did not warn inform Captain Saville of *Hampshire*. That was the first mystery of the sinking.

It was around eight in the evening that *Hampshire* struck a mine about a mile and a half offshore, somewhere between the Brough of Birsay and Marwick Head, although there were claims that it may have been two mines chained together. The explosion ripped her keel apart, jammed the helm and damaged the ships electrics so that the crew could not launch the lifeboats. As the men frantically threw Carley Floats into the leaping sea, *Hampshire* began to sink.

The cry 'Make way for Lord Kitchener!' sounded, and sweating, fearful men stepped aside as the erect, iron-eyed soldier marched through the brown smoke, his greatcoat flapping around his legs. As *Hampshire* sank in around fifteen minutes, Kitchener was last seen on deck, talking calmly with members of his personal staff. Only twelve men managed to scramble ashore on Orkney, and the body of Kitchener was never recovered.

With the sinking occurring so close to shore, many Orcadians were aware precisely what happened, but now came the second mystery of the day. The Postmistress at Birsay telegraphed the Royal Navy at Kirkwall: 'Battlecruiser seen in distress between Marwick Head and the Brough of Birsay.' At once the crew of the Stromness Lifeboat begged permission to launch and save the lives of the men struggling in the water. The naval authorities refused, and, it is said, even neglected to pass on information so hindering the local people who wished to help those men who were trying to swim ashore. Some claimed that soldiers marched to the coast, their bayoneted rifles preventing the Orcadians from helping the stricken seamen. It certainly seems true that those survivors who reached Orkney were hustled away from the press, and perhaps kept apart in far-flung postings.

There seem to be further mysteries about the sinking of *Hampshire*. The release of official documents about the sinking was delayed, or possibly permanently stopped, and the names of some of Kitchener's staff were allegedly not placed on the Commonwealth War Graves Commission register. The mystery of *Hampshire* has never satisfactorily been resolved: why did she race north in such adverse conditions? Why was her captain not informed of the possibility of mines? Why was the lifeboat not allowed to sail, and why the soldiers along the cliffs?

Some theorists claim that Kitchener was never on board and that a double was killed in his place. Others thought that the government no longer considered Kitchener an asset, but a liability who had to be removed. The answer will probably never be known.

Although the death of Kitchener remains enigmatic, there were thousands of other tragedies in that most terrible of all wars. Some were on a massive scale, such as the slaughter on the first day of the Somme, others were smaller, but just as terrible to the people involved. One involved a fishing boat from Arbroath.

THE FISHING BOAT

MAGGIE SMITH

Sitting in Arbroath's Signal Tower Museum, the wooden plaque is very simple and very direct. It commemorates a local fishing boat, *Maggie Smith*, which was lost on 9th February 1918. There are three names inscribed on the plaque: David Cargill, James Beattie, and John Spink, names as familiar to the fishermen of Arbroath as waves to the sea that beats against the harbour wall. Generations of men have carried these names to the fishing grounds of Cockennie Reef and the Bell Rock. To the fishing families of Angus, death was a familiar visitor. It lurked at the harbour bar of Arbroath, it waited in the sudden North Sea squall, it lay hidden at night, watching for the collision of working boats and it sat quietly in the heavy sea boots that could drag a fisherman down. Three steps and over was the fisherman's walk, for there was no space on the deck of a traditional Scottish fishing boat and a man in iron-studded boots could not swim in the chilly North Sea.

A fisherman's death was always tragic in the close-knit communities along the coast, but death had many allies in 1918. The Great War had started in August 1914 and was proving as murderous at sea as on land; around one in four British merchant vessels were lost each trip, while great grey warships had smashed each other to pieces with massive shells. The North Sea was about the most dangerous water in the world for merchant seamen. There were the sinister submarines that slithered out of the water to pour shell after shell into unarmed fishing boats, and the roistering surface warships that could smash a drifter in seconds. Worst of all, perhaps, were the mines, moored as defensive positions or simply left to float with the tide and collide with the hull of any passing vessel. The last thing many seamen saw was the devil's horns of a mine protruding from the water. Others saw nothing at all.

It may have been like that for the crew of *Maggie Smith*. She was a motor liner, owned and normally skippered by James Smith of Union Street East in Arbroath, who regularly sailed with his son, also named James. On Friday the 8th February, neither of the Smiths had baited their lines, so there was no point in going to sea. These lines were around a mile long, with a hook every yard or so. Each hook had to be baited, generally with one or more mussels, and although it was the men who went to sea, it was their women who did the dirty, time-consuming work of baiting. Perhaps the women had not been able to find bait that day, or more likely there had been a previous agreement that David Cargill should sail that Saturday.

It is common in wartime for the Royal Navy to commandeer merchant shipping for its own use. Dundee whalers were commandeered in the French wars, motor launches used for commando raids in the Second World War, cruise liners for troop carrying in the Falklands War. The Great War was no exception; the Navy commandeered hundreds of fishing boats, including David Cargill's steam drifter. For over three years Cargill sailed in the Straits of Dover, dubbed 'Suicide Corner' because of the high casualty rate, no doubt yearning for the war to end. A photograph of him exists, showing a handsome, bearded man, proud in his Naval uniform. He came home to Arbroath on leave while the navy refitted his boat and returned to his real job of fishing. It must have been a relief for him to sail the familiar waters off Arbroath, and he had a good crew in *Maggie Smith*.

John Spink was another local man, coming from South Street. If there is such a thing as a typical

Arbroath face, John Spink possessed it. He looks out from his photograph, steady-eyed beneath the ubiquitous cap, with a small black moustache above a firm mouth. The third member of the crew was little more than a boy; his name was James Beattie, and he was also of South Street.

Maggie Smith was a twenty-eight-year-old, Arbroath built two-masted lugger, fully decked and with a thirty horsepower Kelvin diesel engine. It was five in the morning when she left Arbroath harbour, crossing the bar, and heading out toward Bell Rock. It was dark at that time on a February morning, and as it was wartime, all the boats sailed without lights and in a single line. Immediately astern of *Maggie Smith* was *Caller Ou*, skippered by Bill Eaton. About three-quarters of an hour after leaving harbour there was a tremendous explosion directly ahead of *Caller Ou*, and the boat was steering through a litter of debris. Bill Eaton stopped the engines and swept the area for survivors, but in the dark could see nothing. There was also the fear that a German submarine might be watching through his periscope, so Eaton returned to Arbroath to report.

The Royal Navy patrolled the Bell Rock fishing ground and sent a vessel to investigate the scene of the explosion, but again there was no sign of survivors. Two days later Frederick Fraser, the Fishery Officer at Montrose, wrote: 'it has just been reported to me that one of the Arbroath motor line boats was sunk on Saturday by a submarine, and the crew is still missing.'

While some people suspected that the boat had hit a mine, others believed that a submarine had surfaced and blown up *Maggie Smith*. Submarines were known to operate off the Scottish East Coast, for early in the war a submarine had surfaced near a fishing boat and pirated the catch. 'Be thankful that I am a kind-hearted man' the German commander had said, 'or I would have sent you to the bottom.' In September 1916, a German submarine had also sunk the Gourdon fishing boat *Bella* off Tod Head. Until October that year, the relatives believed that a mine had sunk the boat, and there must have been a great relief when they learned that the five-man crew had been taken as prisoners to Germany.

Most of the local fishermen, however, believed that a mine had destroyed *Maggie Smith*. Many of the requisitioned fishing boats were used to sweep for mines, which had become a significant weapon in the naval war. In March 1917, the Germans had moored mines off Red Head, between Arbroath and Montrose, until a local fishing boat had reported them, and the Royal Navy cleared the area. In his later report to the Fishery Board in Edinburgh, Frederick Fraser said that *Maggie Smith* was 'either sunk by a submarine or blown up by striking a mine' however he added that 'had a submarine been there no doubt more of the boats would have been sunk.'

German records indicate that there was no submarine in the area on that date, but that UC-49 laid five mines around the Bell Rock on the 25th January, two of which were between Arbroath and the fishing ground. It is most likely that *Maggie Smith* fell victim to one of these German mines. Nonetheless, there was also a British minefield in St Andrews Bay, and it is possible that the current carried a drifting mine toward the Bell Rock. Overall, the evidence points to a German mine sinking the Arbroath boat, although there was still hope that the crew had been taken prisoner.

Out of respect for the missing men, the Arbroath boats did little fishing the next week, and nearly a month later the Admiralty informed their families that the crew of *Maggie Smith* might be held prisoner in Germany. Unfortunately, they were not; the three men never returned home.

Other local fishing boats were also lost in that war. In 1914 Dundee had a fleet of twelve trawlers, but by July 1917 the enemy had sunk four. One of the worst disasters was *Primrose*, which was sunk, with all nine crew on 5th February 1917. The men left thirty-two dependants, the silent sufferers of the war. Two months later another was sunk, although that time the crew was saved.

Nevertheless, fishermen were quite capable of striking back, given the correct weapons and equipment. Around ten thousand Scottish fishermen served in either the Royal or the Merchant Navy during the Great War, many in patrol boats or on minesweepers. In August 1917, the armed trawlers *Jacinta, Thomas Young,* and *Chirkara* sunk the German submarine UB 41 off the Firth of Tay, while five months later the trawlers *W.S.Bailey* and *Fort George* sunk UB-63 in the Forth. Fishermen contributed a great deal to winning the war, and the Fishermen's Memorial at London's Tower Bridge is only one memorial to their sacrifice. The Signal Tower Museum at Arbroath overlooks the sea where the crew of *Maggie Smith* made their last voyage, and the small wooden plaque is a more homely, and perhaps more fitting, memorial to the local men.

When that war ended in 1918, Europe enjoyed twenty-one years of precarious peace before the next round with a rejuvenated Germany began. By then Adolf Hitler and the Nazis had set Europe against itself and Scotland, once again, was in the front line.

THE PERILOUS BOATS

THE SHETLAND BUS

Shetland is unique. It is an island group that humanity has occupied since Neolithic times, and which contains a fantastic number of archaeological sites. Most of its history is irrevocably lost, but what is known would be quite enough to keep any medium-sized country happy, let alone a small group of islands that is often reluctantly squeezed onto the map of Scotland. From Stone Age settlements to Vikings, the Hanseatic League and whalers, Shetland has seen them all, yet few periods of Shetland's history can compare with the sheer drama and heroism of the years between 1939 and 1945.

In common with the rest of Scotland, Shetland was at war with Nazi Germany from September 1939, and in November that year, six German bombers bombed and machine-gunned the harbour, sinking a flying boat that was moored there. However, it was in spring of 1940 that the islands were thrust straight into the front line. The German invasion of Norway caught Britain unprepared, but a hurriedly gathered expeditionary force sailed to help Norwegian resistance. Ill-equipped and poorly prepared, the British were pushed out of Norway, and on the 10th June 1940 Norway surrendered. Although the Germans had occupied their country, many Norwegians determined to continue fighting. Shetland also took steps to combat a possible invasion, with troops shipped to the islands and defences prepared in case the Germans should try to invade.

It was not long before determined Norwegians took to the old Viking routes, crossing the dangerous sea to Shetland in small boats. In 1940 alone, 30 boats brought more than 200 people to the islands. Some were refugees, others sailed to Shetland purely to be trained and equipped for a fighting return, for the Norwegian resistance was among the most ferocious of any during the war. Indeed, combined with the raids of British Commandos and the perceived threat of a British counter-invasion, the Norwegian resistance tied down ten German divisions which could well have turned the tide in Normandy, Italy, North Africa, or Russia.

PIRATES AND PICKLED HEADS

Less concerned with aggressive warfare than with helping the desperate refugees, the people of Shetland extended so friendly a hand that in 1944 the Norwegian Government in Exile mentioned: 'the excellent reception which has been indicated by every newcomer who has passed through Shetland. They have met with kindness and understanding by everyone they have been in contact with, and for this, we are very grateful.'

Always ready to cause trouble for the Nazis, Britain created a dynamic organisation in Shetland. Two officers came to Lunna House, on the northeast coast of Shetland's Mainland, supported by a group of hardy sergeants and two score Norwegian sailors. In time they built up a formidable armament and began a two-way ferry service to Norway. While escapees and frustrated young men sailed one way, highly trained operatives, arms, and saboteurs returned, determined to be a sharp thorn in the Nazi hide.

The following year the organisation moved to Scalloway, still in Shetland, where there were better facilities for repairing the boats that so often returned damaged. The local engineering firm of William Moore and Sons proved adept and ready to keep the boats running, a slipway was built for the service and named after Prince Olaf of Norway, who visited in October 1942.

The passage between Shetland and Norway was

so frequent that it became known as the Shetland Bus, and the Norwegian seamen who braved storms, bitter cold, and the Germans were every bit as daring as their Viking ancestors. In the early stages, they used old wooden fishing boats, and losses were heavy, with six vessels lost to enemy action or the weather. However, when somebody suggested that the bus service should be stopped, and the seamen drafted into the Free Norwegian Navy, the bus operators refused. 'Give us better boats, they demanded' and we will carry on the fight.'

Better boats were produced, thanks to the generosity of the United States; three much faster and heavily armed United States submarine chasers that were capable of fighting off even attacking German aircraft. Naming them *Hessa*, *Vigra*, and *Hitra* after three Norwegian islands, the Norwegian seamen continued the bus service, with far fewer casualties.

Probably as important as the passage of men and material was the impact on Norwegian morale. As long as the Shetland Bus continued, they knew that they were not alone. They knew the people of Shetland, closely connected to Norway by blood and heritage, were thinking of them, and by association, so was the rest of Britain.

The crossings were hazardous. Because of the German patrols, the most extended voyages could last for weeks in boats only fifty feet long. From late in 1940, and always through the worst of the winter months, the bus kept hope alive. It is hard to imagine the conditions: appalling weather, no lights, and always the danger of mines, submarines, aircraft, or German surface vessels. Some of the bus operators, such as Leif Larsen, perhaps better known as Shetland Larsen, were true heroes. Larsen slipped free of Norway in February 1941 aboard a fishing smack, saying that he 'didn't very much like the Germans walking around the streets' of his hometown. Trained in Britain, he was elected as skipper and became the best known of all the seamen of the Shetland Bus. Shipwrecked twice, he was decorated more than any other naval seaman as he survived an amazing fifty-two bus trips between Shetland and Norway.

Possibly the most memorable was his Traena expedition of March 1943 when he was delivering arms to a resistance group. With that mission successfully completed, Larsen was attacked on the return voyage. Two German planes dived on his boat, hitting six of the eight men on board. Larsen and the survivors took to the lifeboat and after four days at sea were rescued by a Royal Navy Motor Torpedo Boat (MTB) from Shetland.

Kare Iversen was another of the Norwegian bus men. He was twenty-one when the Germans invaded his country, already an experienced seaman, and he joined the resistance. When the Germans realised that he was dangerous to them, he borrowed his father's forty-two-foot boat, gathered a trio of like-minded men, and set off for Shetland. Iversen left at night, for the German patrol boat retired at eight in the evening, and he sailed without lights. On the third day of their voyage, they survived a prolonged attack by a German flying boat, but continued, arriving safely at Sandwick. A few days later he was en-route for London and training. He returned to Shetland to take part in active operations that lasted until the end of the war.

With ties between Norway and Scotland always steady, it is not surprising that there were romances between the Norwegian seamen and Shetland women, but even the girls were not supposed to know when the buses would sail. Iversen, for example, was married to a Shetland girl.

'We're off on a fishing trip,' the Norwegians would say, but nobody was fooled as the tiny boats sailed west, toward Nazi-dominated Europe. The women would watch, as Shetland women have always watched their men sail to sea or to war and would wonder and worry.

Not every trip was a success as the Germans had a supply of traitors—quislings-on whom they depended for information. Many members of the Norwegian Resistance ended in the hands of the

Gestapo, to endure hideous torture and death. Fully aware of the activities of the Shetland Bus, the German authorities in Berlin ordered that it be halted. After two resistance fighters landed by Shetland Bus and shot an officer of the Gestapo, the Germans took their revenge on the village of Telavag. They removed the entire male population to a concentration camp and placed the women and children in an internment camp before razing the village to the ground. Horror followed horror as the Germans tried to destroy the resistance network, but the Norwegians fought on, and the bus continued to run.

The Shetland Bus is remembered in Norway and in Shetland. Forty-four of the busmen died, but nobody will ever know how many lives they saved, or by how long they shortened the war. It was a section of Scottish nautical history that deserves to be better remembered. However, even in the darkest days of war there have been lighter moments, and sometimes even the loss of a ship can have some compensation for somebody…

THE LEGEND

POLITICIAN

It has been a feature of the nautical wars of the last couple of centuries that the Scottish islands have provided a disproportionate number of quality seamen. That islanders should also be seamen seems almost natural, but the cost to small communities when even a single ship goes down is tragic. The loss of two or three fit young men to a tiny village is often irreparable.

The Second World War was no exception. When HMS *Rawalpindi*, an ex-P&O Liner with limited armament, steamed to protect a convoy in November 1939, twelve of her crew were from Lewis. *Rawalpindi*, under Captain Kennedy, met the German battlecruisers ship *Scharnhorst* and *Gneisenau* in appallingly unequal combat between Iceland and the Faroe Islands. With chivalry that should be remembered, the German warships signalled the heavily outgunned ex-passenger liner to heave to and abandon ship. Kennedy refused. The battle was short, and *Rawalpindi* went down with honour. There were thirty-eight survivors. Eight of the twelve Lewismen were killed.

About a year later the Eagle Oil tanker *San Demetrio*, carrying twelve thousand tons of high-octane petrol, was set alight by the German pocket battleship *Admiral Scheer* despite the gallantry of another armed merchant cruiser *Jervis Bay*. The tanker was abandoned but after a few days in mid-Atlantic one lifeboat's crew sighted *San Demetrio* drifting, still afire but afloat. Able Seaman Calum MacNeil sailed the lifeboat back to the tanker, and the men boarded the stricken ship.

With difficulty, the seamen extinguished the fires, fitted emergency steering, and set the engines running again. All *San Demetrio* lacked was charts and a compass; and there was the small matter of some hundreds of miles of Atlantic to cross, where U-boats and surface raiders could still be hunting. However, Second Officer Hawkins steered them first to Ireland then, under a naval escort, to the Clyde. AB Calum MacNeil and AB Roddie MacLennan shipped home to Barra where they found a new hardship created by war. A whisky shortage—and MacLennan was due to be married.

However, island life can have some advantages,

and occasionally even war can provide some compensation…

On a February evening in 1941, with heavy rain and thick fog adding to the usual navigational difficulties of Hebridean waters, the Liverpool registered *Politician* of around twelve thousand tons suddenly slammed aground. Perhaps the navigating officer had thought he was approaching the Sound of Barra, the stretch of water between Barra and Eriskay; instead, he was further north and had entered the Sound of Eriskay, between Eriskay and South Uist.

As the captain had discovered, this passage was unsuitable for large vessels, being narrow and, at least at low tide, only two fathoms deep. The bad weather only made things worse. As soon as she struck, on a rock to the east of the ten-acre islet of Calvay, *Politician* sounded her siren. The din awakened the good people of Eriskay, sent seagulls into a frenzy, and started dogs barking the length and breadth of the island.

In those nervous times, some people may have thought that the Germans had landed, but the islanders hurried to the shore, lanterns swinging, to find the source of the noise. There was astonishment, probably mingled with sympathetic dismay, as they saw the great cargo ship stranded barely a hundred yards offshore. Small boats were launched; *Politician's* crew rescued and brought

PIRATES AND PICKLED HEADS

ashore to be treated with the tremendous hospitality of the Hebrides.

For a few weeks, *Politician* lay neglected on her rock, but she was not forgotten. Men whispered that she carried thousands of bottles as cargo; bottles of whisky for export to the United States; good quality whisky; top brands like Edradour and Johnny Walker. Eyes would swivel and fix on the hapless *Politician*, stranded with no crew and a valuable cargo, and people might mention SS *Jamaica Progress*. She had been torpedoed a mile offshore with a load of bananas and spirit of rum. None of the rum had come ashore, but *Politician* was closer, ashore, and available.

'Remind me,' men might say: 'what are the rules of salvage? And is there not a whisky shortage in the islands?'

Men from Eriskay launched their boats, hoisted the single lugsail, or hauled at the oars. They boarded the freighter, searched; found and realised they were in heaven. The stories were true if a little understated. *Politician* was full of whisky, by the bottle, by the crate—and there was no Exciseman for many miles. There were drawbacks of course; at low water, the ship was too high sided to board. And was this legal?

Time righted the first as *Politician* settled down, enabling men to clamber aboard with some ease. And now the work began as the cargo was taken from the wreck and into the hearts and mouths of the islanders. Small boats clustered round *Politician*, removing whisky by the crate. By day it was easy, by night less so but the native innovation which had helped rescue *San Demetrio* came in useful now. Men with Tilly Lights crammed into the hold, ignoring the oil-filthy water that surged above their knees as they assiduously lightened the cargo.

Boats came from Eriskay, from Barra, from South Uist, and, as word spread, from much further afield. They came from Lewis and Harris, Benbecula, the Small Isles, and the West Highland mainland, they raised sails and crossed the familiar, choppy seas to descend on the Sound of Eriskay and the stranded, slowly emptying *Politician*. With so much so readily available, respect for the whisky quickly eroded. The Water of Life was used as paraffin, poured onto reluctant fires, and used to clean oil and grease from the hands of working men.

Work itself became more pleasant when there was a bottle of whisky waiting at the end of the plough furrow or sitting on the housewife's table. People drank more than they should and greeted the dawn with a different bottle to that with which they had said farewell to the dusk. Broken bottles lay abandoned, with the dumpy hens sipping eagerly at the scorned dregs until they too became inebriated.

PIRATES AND PICKLED HEADS

At last and inevitably the Ministry of Shipping realised that one of their ships was missing and the Customs and Excise bristled with agitation at the thought of all this lost revenue. A brave, perhaps remarkably honest, night watchman was set to guard what remained of the cargo while police and Excisemen launched a joint assault on the fragmented islands with their misbehaving inhabitants. By now Roddy MacLennan had enjoyed his wedding. No doubt he was back at sea, serving, and saving his country, braving torpedoes and storms.

With the police on the prowl, the ingenuity of the Hebrideans was thoroughly tested. As so many of their young men risking their lives for their country, were they not entitled to the salvage of a wreck? Apparently not; authority demanded its revenue.

Miraculously the whisky began to disappear; hidden in discreet caches in seldom-visited locations the length and breadth of the western Highland seaboard. The Hebridean intelligence service warned when officialdom was approaching, and the golden bottles were secreted away. Some were thrust deep into the heather thatch in the manner of broadswords after the 1715 Rising, others hung from hooks in the smoke-black chimneys or were buried under the potatoes. The islanders even nestled whisky bottles inside mattresses, or in peat stacks. Whisky was poured into the stone hot water bottles or placed in bed beside normally agile but suddenly sick and frail old men. Most though, still in the original cases, was taken by the flickering light of lanterns to be buried in the vacant moor, or by the friendly, watchful, sea.

To locate their prey, the Excisemen would have to dig up half the Hebrides.

Ponderous but efficient, officialdom reacted. A salvage tug chugged out to Calvay and hauled Politician off her rock, after which she was sliced in half. The aft section could not be recovered and was sunk in the Sound, while the fore section was towed to Lochboisdale and, eventually, to the Clyde.

Retribution followed. Some of the islanders were taken to the court at Lochmaddy and charged with various offences against the Customs and Excise. Sentenced to a month or two in Inverness jail, they were well-treated, and on their return would probably dig up a bottle from their concealed cache to celebrate their freedom.

There was a cheerful toast current in the Isles:

'Health to the one who did not see Calvay.'

On Eriskay and Barra, the salvagers could sit and watch the oldsters of the island experiment with the bicycles that had also been part of *Politician's* cargo. As was the toothpaste young boys enjoyed squirting at each other. And all the time other Hebrideans were crewing the ships that carried such cargoes, keeping open the seaways of the Free World.

In 1990 an ex-US Navy tug, *Whisky Warrior*, sailed from Leith to the Sound of Eriskay. As support ship for a diving barge, she supervised the recovery of the whisky that had remained on the aft section of Politician. However, seawater had contaminated such bottles as were recovered and the contents were undrinkable.

But the story remains as fresh as ever, and the only pub on Eriskay is called, most suitably: Politician.

While the story of *Politician* is well-kent, there were other treasure ships off Scotland, and another cargo whose fate was decided by outside events.

THE TREASURE CARRIER

PRINCE CHARLES

There are few more evocative figures in Scottish history than Charles Edward Stuart, the Bonnie Prince. His story is well known; the landing in Scotland with seven men, raising the standard at Glenfinnan, the victories at Prestonpans, Clifton, and Falkirk, the carnage at Culloden and the romanticised wanderings through the heather. Less well known is the treasure that Charlie left behind. Or, more accurately, the treasures that he never received. Folklore and legend tell of at least two treasures, and folklore and legend can be disturbingly accurate in the Highlands.

In April 1746 two French frigates, *Mars* and *Bellone*, left the port of Nantes and steered for

Scotland. Rather than carrying reinforcements for the then defeated Jacobite army, both vessels held stores, probably arms and ammunition, and gold. The Jacobites were always short of munitions of war and the French ever willing to create disharmony in Britain. Although the Royal Navy was patrolling for just such incursions, the art of blockade was not yet perfected and the French vessels managed to slip into Loch Nam Uamh on the Scottish West Coast, where a party of Jacobites was waiting. By now it was early May, and Culloden had been fought, the army of the Prince scattered.

The stores were landed, small boats rowing to the beach, darkened lanterns guiding them in as the strained men in silk and tartan watched hill and sea for Hanoverians. The Royal Navy arrived, sailing up the loch in time to interrupt the disembarkation. Ignoring the heaped-up supplies on the beach, His Majesty's Ships *Terror*, *Baltimore*, and *Greyhound* moved into the attack; it was better for the Navy to fight the French than fire on the remnants of a failed rising and the deep batter of naval gunfire echoed from the Highland hills. Either unwilling to fight or outgunned by the British, the French ships fled with the Royal Navy in pursuit, leaving the stores and gold on the shore.

There is no clear account of the fate of this

treasure. One story says that the MacDonalds of Barrisdale kept about 800 Louis d'Or and carried the rest, perhaps another 35,000 Louis d'Or in six barrels, to a patch of forest near Loch Arkaig. Later somebody moved a portion of this to the southern shore of the loch, near Achnacarry. At a meeting later that month, a quantity of gold was issued to the clan chiefs, but more was buried somewhere in Glen Gamgarry. Another story says that the MacLeans helped dispose of the gold.

Whatever the truth, if that treasure was ever fully recovered the finder kept the fact very quiet. And if not, there may be a sizeable fortune waiting at Loch Arkaig, or Glen Gamgarry. Perhaps the French were very liberal with their wealth, or the amount of Louis d'Or they distributed has grown in the telling, for another substantial quantity had been landed only a couple of months earlier.

That story began in November of the previous year when French shipping had been using the port of Montrose. This was a known Jacobite haven; a mainly Episcopalian town rife with smuggling, so the government had no qualms in sending HMS *Hazard*, a 16-gun sloop, as a deterrent. On the 13th, Captain Hill hove to off Ferryden and ordered his guns run out. For those townsfolk near the waterside, that must have been an ominous sight. Only after three days of bombardment did Hill discover that there were neither French nor Jacobite soldiers in Montrose. But lying at the quay were a couple of ships whose masters had piloted in the French, and in a deserted coastal fort were some useful cannon.

Burning the pilot ships, Hill removed the cannon from the fort and placed them on a vessel named *Owners Goodwill* at the quay.

Hazard remained at Ferryden for another few days, when a small French warship came into the harbour with 150 soldiers on board. These were Scots in French service, plus several Irishmen and some artillery for the Jacobites. The Frenchman grounded at the harbour mouth, trapping *Hazard* inside, and the two vessels battered each other with cannon fire. The gun battle continued as the Jacobites stripped *Owners Goodwill* of her cannon and dragged them up the small but prominent eminence of Horologue Hill. In the dark of the winter night, the Jacobites set up their battery and fired on *Hazard*. The scene was dramatic, if deadly, long tongues of flame dancing around Montrose, reflecting eerily on the black water, and choking smoke rolling down the broad high street of the town. In the morning, either exhausted or out of ammunition, Captain Hill surrendered. This Jacobite capture of a Royal Navy sloop was a small victory but might have proved significant for its propaganda value alone.

And the excitement at Montrose had not

finished. *Le Fine*, a French frigate, appeared and disembarked three hundred more men for Charlie's army. Again these were Scots fighting for France. Then came the 40-gun HMS *Milford*. Another battle began, with both ships running aground in the tricky river mouth and the French landing 12-pounders to hammer at the British ship. But the Royal Navy is not easily defeated, and when a shore party hauled *Milford* off the sandbank with minutes to spare, her captain outfought and defeated *Le Fine*.

In the meantime *Hazard* had slipped out to sea and over to France. Commanded by the Montrose seaman William Lesslie and renamed *Prince Charles*, she joined the Jacobite cause. In March 1746, loaded with supplies and gold for the beleaguered Jacobite army, *Prince Charles* was sighted off Troup Head by HMS *Sheerness*, one of the ubiquitous Royal Navy frigates. Outgunned, Prince Charles fled through the stormy Pentland Firth but, heavier and better able to cope with the conditions, *Sheerness* caught the Jacobite sloop off the Kyle of Tongue. Lesslie attempted to use the frigate's greater size and weight against her. If *Prince Charles* could sail over the sandbanks that acted as a barrier at the entrance of the Kyle, the heavier *Sheerness* might not be able to follow.

However, these were unfamiliar, tricky waters and at Ard Skinid, *Prince Charles* ran aground. Stuck there, she had no reply to the heavy broadsides poured in by *Sheerness* until the ebbing tide forced the frigate to seek deeper water. By then *Prince Charles* had been mortally damaged, with her fragile planking splintered and her crew decimated. As it was pointless to stay and they were unable to sail out, the Jacobites decided to abandon ship.

That night, with the Navy frigate hovering somewhere offshore, the survivors of *Prince Charles* carried their cargo ashore and headed south along the coast of the kyle. It would be an interesting picture, the heavily laden men in knee breeches or wide canvas sea trousers, the cold water of the Atlantic lapping at the stricken sloop and the glances out to sea in case the lurking frigate should send a landing party. Melness House was handy, home to a friendly Mackay and after a night here the survivors headed south again, along the shore to Kinloch and then inland to Loch Hakon. And there they were ambushed. This was Mackay land and save for the Laird of Melness, Clan Mackay strongly supported the Hanoverians. With the Highland intelligence service so efficient, news of a naval battle soon spread, and Mackay of Reay knew about the fugitives in his land. Earlier that year Lord Loudon's Foot had been defeated at Dornoch by the Jacobites, and eighty redcoats had retreated to Tongue House. Now was their chance for revenge as Mackay of Reay led them, reinforced by some of his own followers, to face the seamen of *Prince Charles*.

They met at Druim Na Corpa. Three of the Jacobites were killed; the remainder scattered, throwing most of the gold into Loch Hakon. Although over 12,000 golden Louis d'Or were recovered, the balance, perhaps 15,000 pieces of gold, has never been found. It could still be in the loch. Local legend tells of the occasional coin turning up, found by a shepherd or a fisherman. There is even a tale of a cow coming home with a gold coin stuck to her hoof but where is the remainder?

Unlike many other Jacobites, Lesslie was released. His papers proved he was no traitor—if any were—but a 'French pilot in the service of His Most Christian Majesty Louis XIV'. Next year he was back at sea, trading salmon to Dunkirk in *Marjory* of Montrose. Did he know of the gold? Of course—but did he make an attempt at recovery? Perhaps not. The Highlands were in a very disturbed state with redcoat soldiers creating havoc, burning, looting, and killing. Those who had participated in the rising possibly thought it better to keep their heads down and say nothing.

Over a century later, the world had altered. Great Britain had lost much of her American empire and gained another in India, and there was civil war in the United States. As men of the same blood destroyed each other with fratricidal hatred, the northern states imposed a naval blockade on the southern. As in every war there are a few gainers; in this instance it was a family of jute manufacturers in Dundee.

THE CLIPPER

LOCHEE

When people think of Dundee, it is quite likely that the first phrase that comes to mind is 'Jute, Jam and Journalism', even although the city has altered and diversified to a tremendous degree since that was accurate. At one time, however, Dundee was the jute capital of the world, and among the most influential of the Jute Barons was the Cox family of Lochee.

Even today the name of Cox is still spoken daily, perhaps because of the great tall chimney, 'Cox's Stack' that rises high above the community of Lochee, dwarfing the nearby car park and casting its historic shadow over local housing. At the end of the nineteenth century, this entire area was a major industrial centre, with Cox's Works employing five thousand people. *Lochee* was the hub of a worldwide operation that stretched from Calcutta to the American West, so the noise from the looms that clattered beneath the Stack never ended. At Lochee, the Cox Works could bring in raw jute on its own railway and transport out a finished product that was used for tents, tarpaulins and canopies, sacking and floor covering and a thousand other things.

In the 1860s, the Cox kingdom was still expanding, feeding on the wars that required tents and gun covers, and the gold diggers who also needed tents, and canopies of Dundee jute covered the great wagon trains that opened up the American West. Until that time all the Cox jute was exported on chartered vessels, but when James Cox was in London during the 1860s, he had the germ of an idea. The American Civil War was at its height, and with the Federal Navy in the ascendancy, many ships from the Confederate States were seeking shelter in British ports.

At that time, ships from North America were renowned for their speed and beauty. They were sleek, fast, and efficient so that while many British carriers bought their vessels from yards in Nova Scotia and New Brunswick in British North America, American ships carried a large percentage of world trade. The Navigation Acts limited the size and proportions of British vessels, so they were too short and too ponderous. Ships from the United

States dominated the Atlantic passage, and ships from the United States swooped over to China to collect the cargoes of tea. By the 1860s Britain had fought back, with British-built clippers showing even the Americans how to race home, but American ships still carried the reputation of excellence.

When James Cox saw one of these American beauties sheltering in London, he realised that his Lochee kingdom did not have a navy. Without his own ships, he had to pay freight charges to other companies, so handing out a part of his fortune to give others a more considerable profit margin. If he owned the ships, he could cut costs, sail where and when he chose and surely enhance his finances. There were many tall ships in London, but only one captured his attention. She was a queen of the waves; an 1800-ton Southern belle clipper named *Cherubim*.

Cherubim so impressed James Cox that he bought her immediately. With her name changed to *Lochee*, a new figurehead to guide her through the seas, and the most modern equipment that money could buy, the first jute clipper of Dundee proudly sailed to sea. From Dundee, *Lochee* voyaged to Calcutta, sliding through the waves with such speed that people remarked on her passage. She lingered long enough in the Hooghly to pick up a cargo of jute and headed back to Dundee, down the

Indian Ocean, round the Cape of Storms and up the length of the Atlantic. The Tay was welcoming, the taverns of Fish Street ready to accept the hot coppers of the crew, and it seemed that there was a brand-new beginning for Dundee. Rather than shipping with carriers and sharing the profits with intermediaries, the Dundee textile barons would own their shipping and rattle the take into their tills.

James Cox, however, was not so sure. Although *Lochee* was a lovely ship and had made a fast passage, he wrote in his journal that 'she left little profit in consequence of the large sum paid on her outfit.' The Cox family was not renowned for wasting money, so *Lochee* was soon sailing again. Picking up a cargo of coal from Tayport, she was off again to the East. Coal was not the most popular of cargoes to carry, for it tended to shift in boisterous weather. Indeed, of the 264 British ships of 300 tons and over that had vanished between 1881 and 1883, 86 had carried coal. If the cargo shifted, the ship could develop a list, the crew would labour at the pumps, but after a while, the pumps would be fouled with coal dust and would fail. Ships with heavy bulk cargoes did not float for long when they capsized.

Perhaps some of the crew pondered on the dangers as they hoisted sail and passed the sandbars at the mouth of the Tay. More likely they nursed their hangovers; thought of the women they left behind and pulled mightily on the halyards.

'O Whisky is the life of man
   Whisky Johnny!
   O whisky is the life of man
   And its whisky for my Johnny!'

The Scottish dockers were used to loading ships with coal. The cargo did not shift, but something else happened. Carrying coal can be hazardous in any condition; even in cold weather, coal, when exposed to air, can produce a measure of heat. In normal circumstances, the heat is created slowly and dissipates quickly, but not all coals are the same; some react quicker than others do. If small pieces, or even dust, of these high-reaction coals, are stored in bulk, with a large surface area, and the heat thus produced cannot escape, spontaneous combustion is possible. Coal stored in the hold of a ship on a long voyage in tropical heat is ideal for this process. Perhaps it was spontaneous combustion, or maybe James Cox was correct when he said that 'the hold had got full of gas' but whatever the cause, there was a major explosion in the hold when *Lochee* was approaching Ceylon (now Sri Lanka). By a miracle, only two of the crew was lost, with all the others saved, but the accident ended the interest of James Cox in shipping, at least for a while. It was not the fault of the ship's master, nor the owners; between 1875 and 1883, fifty-seven coal carriers caught fire, with the loss of the ship. A further 328 coal-carrying ships went missing in the same period. Coal was just a hazardous cargo.

James Cox had sewn the seed with *Lochee*, but the harvest came in an entire fleet of clippers. The next in the Cox dynasty, *William Cox* was of the same brood, but rather than owning a single ship; he spread his money. Ownership of shipping was divided into shares, each one being one 64th of the value of a ship. Most vessels were owned by a group of several people, each with a minimum of one share. William Cox had shares in many vessels, from the steamers of the Dundee, Perth, and London Line, to the sturdy ships that sailed to the Arctic. In 1874 he was one of the partners in the Dundee Clipper Line, most of whose fifteen vessels first kissed salt water when they slid down from a Dundee shipyard. It is heartening to know that the first ship of the Dundee Clipper Line was launched from Alexander Stephen's yard at Marine Parade and bore the familiar name *Lochee*. She was also a record breaker, sailing in 1882 from Calcutta to Dundee in just 90 days.

Each one of these clippers was beautiful, each one was distinctive, and each one is worth a book in herself. Someday somebody may write the definitive history of the Dundee Clipper Line, but until then the name must remain a half-forgotten reminder of the time when Dundee clippers sailed from the Tay to the Hooghly and carried emigrants to Melbourne.

The first was *Maulsden*, and again the Cox connection was strong. When the family lived in Lochee, they named their ship after that area; now the heads of the clan were rippling away from their industrial heartland and named their ship after their grand house in the Angus countryside. Like *Lochee*, *Maulsden* was built for the jute trade, and also like *Lochee*, *Maulsden* had another destiny. In 1883, with 500 hopeful emigrants, she sailed from the Clyde to New South Wales in a record-setting 69 days. In years to come, many Dundee ships would be sold to Australian owners; perhaps the impression made by *Maulsden* lingered Down Under.

In 1875 Alexander Stephen and Sons built *Duntrune*, a vessel which they also named after a grand house. Mrs Clementena Graham was the owner of the house of Duntrune, and she had quite a claim to fame. In her youth, she had known the great Admiral Duncan, in her maturity she had written the book Mistification, and now, at 95 years young, she both launched it and modelled the figurehead of Duntrune. As Mrs Graham was also a descendant of Graham of Claverhouse, better known as Bonnie Dundee, she perhaps had the right to name the ship.

Dundee is unique in many things, and her shipping history is no exception. When people speak of the jam, the journalism, or the jute, they often forget all the talent and skill and triumph that these commodities brought to the city. For most of the people that worked in them, the jute factories were a harsh workplace, with hot and heavy toil for little reward. However, the product of these mills helped push forward the boundaries of civilisation, and the ships that carried the jute were amongst the most beautiful that ever sailed. It would be a mistake not to take pride in such beauty, and a larger mistake to forget the skills that brought names native to Dundee to the ports of half the world, which is precisely what vessels such as *Duntrune*, *Maulsden* and *Lochee* did.

These old-time sailing ships, however, were all subject to the whim of wind and weather. One mistake, or one unfortunate combination of circumstances, could render a ship designer's masterpiece into a splintered wreck and toss passengers and crew into a hellish maelstrom of disaster. Such events were bad enough when the ship carried only cargo, but much worse when she was filled with passengers as well.

THE TRAGIC

ANNIE JANE

Vatersay is one of the smaller islands of the Hebrides. It does not have the fame of nearby Barra, from where the pirate MacNeils rowed their galleys, nor does it have the beautiful, haunting song that has made Mingulay known. It is instead a poor small brother, but it has one reminder that perhaps typifies one often forgotten aspect of these seas, and that is their always-present danger.

On the machair overlooking a wide bay of the Atlantic there is a small monument, on which is inscribed:

On the 28th of September 1853, the ship *Annie Jane*, with emigrants from Liverpool to Quebec, was totally wrecked in this bay and three-fourths of the crew and passengers, numbering about 350 men, women, and children, were drowned, and their bodies interred here.

The mid-nineteenth century was the time of the white-sailed emigrant ship when half the world seemed to be on the move as Europe poured out her unwanted or unsettled and ten thousand ships carried them to a new life in the New World. It was a time of folk movement on a scale never before imagined, and Scotland played her part and more than her part. Since the days of Tir-nan-Og, Scots had looked to the western ocean, and although many had travelled eastward for fame and fortune, from the eighteenth century, North America had been the guiding beacon. There had been Scottish colonies in the seventeenth century Americas: Nova Scotia, East New Jersey, Darien, but the westward flood had really started about 1730 and had significantly escalated in the nineteenth century.

It was no luxury cruise to cross the Atlantic in a wind-powered wooden ship. The more unfortunate emigrants travelled 'steerage', which meant they were crammed into a smaller space than was allowed for slaves or convicted criminals, brutally treated, neglected, and despised. Death on the early emigrant ships was common, mainly by disease, for once the emigrants had paid their passage, it hardly mattered to the shipowners or ship master's if they lived or died.

Annie Jane was not one of the worst ships. She

was virtually new, having been built just a few months earlier in Quebec. She was built of prime timber: North American oak and African teak, far superior to many of the so-called 'plantation-built' vessels that were of light pine. With a value of £14,000 and a weight of 1294 tons, *Annie Jane* had been declared A1 at Lloyds. Her Master was every bit as fine as his ship. Captain William Mason was a Master Mariner with thirty-six years of seagoing experience. He was well known, and his peers respected his professional capabilities.

Given an excellent ship and an experienced skipper, there seemed little reason to worry as the emigrants swarmed on board *Annie Jane* that August in 1853. Men, women, and children, they came to Liverpool by train and by carriage, some by steamer from the Clyde and probably the poorest walked for the chance of getting to North America. Most were Scots, but there were also Frenchmen and Germans and the ubiquitous Irish on board, hoping for a better life and prepared to endure the hardships of the crossing in the hope of a brighter future.

Together with the crew, *Annie Jane* had upward of 500 people on board when she slipped her cable and headed west, out of the busy Mersey and into the Irish Sea. There would be a crowd at the dockside to see her depart, relatives of the emigrants who waved goodbye to the loved ones they knew they would probably never see again. Handkerchiefs would flutter in the air, tears would flow, and there would be regrets and sorrow as broken-hearted families were torn asunder, failed by a system that could not allow a decent living for everybody.

Annie Jane had sailed from Quebec to Liverpool in June and was bound to return, working an irregular ferry service across the pond. As well as the emigrants, many of whom would be reeling in the first throes of seasickness, she carried hundreds of tons of iron, 300 tons of general cargo, salt, tea, soap, paper, ropes, and all the other un-romantic commodities that were daily carried by the tall ships. She also had long lengths of railway track, for Canada was building her own railways and Britain supplied much of the materials.

It was the 23rd of August when *Annie Jane* left Liverpool, and after two days of fine sailing, she ran into bad weather. It was night in the Atlantic, with Scotland astern and the long waves hissing along the oaken hull. When the wind began to pick up, the more experienced of the crew knew that they were in for the very devil of a blow. *Annie Jane* continued, but the blow turned into a gale, then a severe gale that howled through the rigging, threw solid chunks of water onboard and hurled the terrified passengers from the wooden shelves on which they were trying to sleep.

Worse came when, with a terrible crash and the rending of cordage, first the fore and then the mizzen topmasts were plucked free. 'Terrible weather' said the calmer of the passengers. 'Terrible cargo stowage' replied those of the crew with enough time to make a comment. But Captain Mason was not daunted; thirty-six years at sea teaches a man endurance as well as patience, so he had the damage repaired and continued the voyage. Morning of the 26th broke with an angry red sky, which by midday developed into a savage squall. Still handicapped by her injuries, *Annie Jane* reacted by pitching more than usual. Few of the passengers understood the sea; they were tradesmen and city people, Glasgow carpenters seeking work with the Canadian Railways, women caring for their children. This terrible experience in a ship they believed already crippled was too much for them. When the storm continued into the night, some drew up a petition and presented it to Captain Mason.

It was apparent that the passengers were unhappy. Not only did they complain about the abysmal conditions on board ship, but they also requested that Captain Mason should return immediately to Liverpool. Petitions at sea were no new idea; the passengers of other ships had presented them in the past and would do in the future. Usually, they were ignored, as this one was.

It is probable that conditions on Annie Jane were no worse than in any other emigrant ship, so Captain Mason would see no reason to alleviate them, if, indeed, he could. After all, the company that owned *Annie Jane* existed to make a profit, and the more passengers she carried, the more money the voyage made. If the captain refused to take all the passengers that he could squeeze in, he jeopardised his position. However, the ship was severely damaged, most of the Atlantic lay ahead, and the cargo had been badly stowed. Pragmatically, Captain Mason put about and headed home.

It was on the 2nd September when *Annie Jane* arrived back in Liverpool. She was a sorry sight, with her mizzenmast a mere stump and her topmasts missing. As soon as she docked, about one hundred passengers disembarked; they had seen enough of the Atlantic and of Annie Jane. Captain Mason set about repairing his ship as some of the remaining passengers sought out the local Government Inspector to complain about conditions on board. Nothing was done; perhaps the inspectors believed that nothing needed to be done and on the 9th of September, after quick repairs, Captain Mason took *Annie Jane* out again.

Now there were officially 450 people on board, but there might have been more for children were calculated as half an adult, and it is possible there were stowaways, desperate to sail to North

America. If the passengers hoped for a more comfortable second trip, they were soon disappointed, for the Atlantic was waiting for them with its fangs bared. On the 12th *Annie Jane* sailed into another gale, and again the passengers were subjected to screaming winds and the rending crash of spars as the fore and mizzen topmasts were carried away, bringing the lower mastheads with them in a terrible tangle of cordage, blocks, and splintered timber. This time Captain Mason brought *Annie Jane* to and executed running repairs while the sea hissed angrily all around. By now even the most optimistic of the passengers were alarmed. With Annie Jane so damaged and the weather deteriorating, there seemed no prospect of a safe Atlantic crossing.

On the 15th of September, a Glasgow cabinetmaker named Ross presented another petition to the captain, recommending that they turn back. But Mason had his professional pride to think of. He could not be seen to bow to the wishes of his passengers. It was a time when the captain was second only to God at sea, and one passenger reported that he said:

'I am the master of this ship. It's Quebec or the bottom, and a bullet for the man who dares to interfere with me in my duty.'

By that time it was a three-cornered duel between the will of the passengers, the will of

Captain Mason and the hunger of the Atlantic. In such a battle there are invariably casualties, and on this occasion, it was *Annie Jane*. The weather did not improve, and at night on the 28th of September, a massive wave burst over the limping ship. It appears that *Annie Jane* was pooped, which meant that a wave landed square on the poop deck, the extreme stern, and surged the whole length of the vessel. The sheer weight of water crushed the poop deck, which collapsed onto the steerage passengers below. Many were killed instantly; others drowned as the seething, freezing water poured in. Within ten minutes Annie Jane was sinking.

As usual in the death of a wooden ship, there were pieces of wreckage floating and tossing on the surface of the sea. Scores of survivors clung to the most considerable portion, a section of the main deck. It would be a terrifying experience, with the darkness of the night, the batter of the sea, the cries of those that could no longer hold on and who were swept away and the knowledge that friends and loved ones were lost. Perhaps the hunger of the sea was sated, for rather than swallow the entire complement of *Annie Jane*, it spat the shocked survivors near to the west sands of Vatersay. They stuck there, with the wreckage trapped within sight of a dark shore, and with terrible seas pounding all around.

When grey dawn seeped light onto the island,

there was some attempt at bringing order out of calamity. The people of Vatersay, rushing to the shore to help, created a causeway out of the wreckage and helped the survivors. Nearly one hundred people crawled off the deck and staggered along the causeway to the island. Another handful had managed to survive the fearful pounding sea to come ashore. In all one hundred and two people survived the wreck, but the shore of Vatersay was a terrible sight.

There were bodies and pieces of bodies, some so mangled as to be unrecognisable. Stunned, cold, shocked, people answered their names to a roll call. It was estimated that 348 people had died in that short space of time. The people of Vatersay did what they could. They dug common graves for the dead and cared for the living as best their scarce resources would allow. A week later the graves were still being excavated, and the Vatersay people were scouring the shore, loading recovered bodies into a pony and trap, and bringing them to their last resting place.

When the surviving Glasgow carpenters saw the bodies of Mr Bell the mate and a French-Canadian priest known as Father Vernier, they fashioned coffins out of the wreckage and gave them a proper burial.

Out of all the horror, one story shines through. Among the passengers were an Irish woman and her two children. She held one child in her arms and tied the second to her back in a tartan shawl. Amongst all the turmoil and terror, she fought for her children's lives. While grown men died in the surf or were torn to pieces on the terrible rocks of Vatersay, this unknown woman survived, and although one of her children died, the other was saved. However, the crew of an equally unknown boat joined this woman in heroism. It appears that the people of Vatersay, or perhaps some early survivors, lit a fire on the beach, and a passing ship send a boatload of men to help. It was an unwritten law of the sea to help those in distress, but in this instance the sea was greedy. Massive waves overturned the boat, while the ship itself was dashed against the steep cliffs at Traidh Varlich. Only the steward survived to tell of the attempted rescue.

Terrible as the loss of *Annie Jane* was, it was only one of the tragedies that marred the sea on Scotland's west coast. It is often on the borders that things go wrong; the places where the sea merges with land, where one country eased into another, or where peace and war are uncertain. It is a truism that there have been more ships wrecked on land than lost without trace at sea, but of all the wrecks off the west of Scotland, none can be more poignant than that of *Iolaire*.

In 1918, after four years of perhaps the most

concentrated bloodshed that the world had ever known, peace had broken out in Europe. The First World War had ended, the Great War, the War to end all Wars and the lads were coming home. From Unst to Penzance the people rejoiced; there would be no more long lists of dead in the newspapers, no more waiting for the dreaded telegram or the knock on the door. Even those who had lost their men were relieved, for their friends, family and neighbours would not have to go through that torment.

Perhaps Lewis had more cause for relief than most, for the island had suffered grievous loss. Lewismen had filled the ranks of the Seaforth Highlanders, one of the regiments that the Germans termed 'Ladies from Hell' because of their valour in battle. But bravery cannot shield a human body from the impact of a machine-gun bullet, and far too many had died in a hundred battles in France and Flanders. At sea, Lewismen had fought at the Battle of the Falklands and at Jutland, they had crewed the darting destroyers that escorted the slow merchant vessels, where Lewismen also served. Now the survivors were coming home, to Park, to Stornoway, to all the little townships and crofts from where they had left to do their bit for Scotland and Empire and freedom.

On the 31st of December 1918, a party of Lewismen had arrived at Kyle of Lochalsh, to be greeted by their jubilant families. There was a mixture there, soldiers in khaki with memories of the terrible trenches, civilians who had crossed the Minch to see them, and the blue-clad sailors. There were wild, happy scenes in Kyle that Hogmanay and so many people that the scheduled mail boat, *Sheila,* could not cope. But the Navy came to the rescue by providing Her Majesty's Yacht *Iolaire* to carry the excess. With the habitual Navy efficiency, the returning servicemen were separated; while the soldiers and civilians crowded onto *Sheila,* the Navy took their own. *Iolaire* was filled with seamen returning home to Lewis.

As so often, the Minch was stormy, but that did not matter. The lads were coming home; ignoring the wild weather, men would be on deck, pointing out the lights of Stornoway and the townships that many thought they would never see again. But darkness and the weather combined to drive *Iolaire* away from the entrance of Stornoway harbour and onto the rocks of the Beasts of Holm. She was only yards from the shore, but in the mounting surf, could have been a hundred miles away for all the help she could get.

Already some men were drowned, but there was a Nessman on board named John MacLeod. While some men leapt into the tormented sea and struck out for shore, to either survive or be dragged under by the undertow, or crushed by the waves, he attached a heaving line to a strong hawser, grabbed the rope and jumped overboard.

MacLeod was a strong swimmer, but the sea pulled at him, tugging him under, smashing high waves against his head. He persevered until he was scrabbling at the weed-covered rocks on the beach. Once there and ignoring the efforts of others to launch boats which could not live in the pounding sea, MacLeod pulled the heaving line, then the hawser ashore and made it fast. Perhaps he shouted to *Iolaire*, or maybe the seamen on board understood what was to be done, but one by one the survivors dragged themselves along the length of the hawser.

Not all made it for the force of the sea dragged men away, or knocked them unconscious, but over seventy men were saved from *Iolaire*, most thanks to the courage of John MacLeod. Two hundred died in the wreck of *Iolaire*, undoubtedly one of the most poignant of all shipwrecks, for men to survive one of the worst wars in history only to be drowned within shouting distance of their home is a bitter irony. They are not forgotten.

Others, victims of their own chiefs, have not been remembered.

THE SLAVE SHIP

WILLIAM

It was 1739 and Scotland was uneasily peaceful. The Black Watch guarded the glens, put down blackmail and whisky smuggling and attracted young men by the glamour of the uniform and the swing of the kilt in the dark Government tartan. There had always been movement from the Highlands, with warriors fighting for their chief in Ireland or for gold in European wars, but now the direction of movement was changing. Rather than south or east, people looked beyond the Western Ocean.

Some had already left their homeland to cross the broad Atlantic. Men of Clan Chattan were in Georgia, defending the frontier against the Spanish and trading with the Creek Indians. Others were bound for the Carolinas, to bring the skirl of the great pipes to the Blue Ridge Mountains and help settle the vast spaces of America. But these were willing emigrants; others who travelled west had no choice in their journey. They had been kidnapped, knocked on the head in some dark alley in Aberdeen or Edinburgh, bound hand and foot and tossed unceremoniously into the hold of a colonial-bound ship. Luckily, such things were restricted only to the Lowland cities; they did not happen in the Gaeltacht.

But conditions in the Highlands were changing rapidly. There was more than Jacobitism to create consternation in the north; new laws curtailed the powers of the Highland chiefs, new industry seeped into the glens, new ideas bothered the heads of the people. Rather than black cattle, money was becoming the unit of currency and the power of a chief was already being reckoned on the size of his bank balance rather than the number of his fighting tail. As their clansmen became less important to them, some chiefs grew cynical. The terrible days of the Clearances were still to come, but even now there were ugly scenes in the north.

Amongst the worst was the time of the *Long Nan Duine*, the 'raider's ship' that stole people away from their homes. MacLeod of Harris and Dunvegan and Sir Alexander MacDonald were the two principal chiefs in Skye, and both were well aware of the world as it was. They would know that their prestige depended on money and that people in the colonies would pay for indentured servants. It must have been a natural step for unprincipled men to use their power to supply this never-ending demand for human muscle. Where individuals could 'nab' a kid or two in the back streets of a city, Highland chiefs could do the same in their lands. After all, if chiefs could use the threat of eviction or worse to compel their followers to war, it was only one step further to force them to servitude. And even easier to use their magisterial powers to claim they were only sending thieves and ne'er-do-wells across the sea. That way no blame could be attached to them.

Of course, the chiefs did not put their reasons in writing. Nobody will ever know the full motive that led to the kidnapping of scores of innocent people, but it seems likely that changing conditions allied to pure greed and abuse of power lay behind what transpired. Either unwilling or unable to perform the deed themselves, the chiefs persuaded Norman MacLeod of Bernera to be hatchet man. Why Norman MacLeod agreed will also never be known. Perhaps he was afraid to argue, or maybe he was a willing partner. Either way, he chartered the ship *William* from Liverpool, loaded it with over one hundred people, half from MacLeod land in Harris and the remainder herded aboard at Loch Bracadale in Sir Alexander MacDonald's Skye.

They would be bewildered, probably frightened, for they had been rounded up with no explanation and little time to prepare. Two hundred years later Hitler's Gestapo would do the same thing to the Jews; but for the Hebrideans, their own chiefs were the persecutors. It was the worst sort of betrayal. MacLeod of Bernera signed himself on board as supercargo and sailed off for the Plantations.

Only a handful of the prisoners had ever been accused of sheep stealing, none of them had faced trial. Certainly, none had been sentenced to transportation. The chiefs stated that they were thieves, but this was blatantly untrue. The vast majority was utterly innocent and just happened to live on the lands of a couple of unscrupulous rogues that abused their power. Fear and worry and perhaps the motion of the ship created sickness, so *William* stopped at Rum and Jura just long enough to unload the unhealthy. After all, no Plantation owner would part with hard cash for damaged goods.

By the time *William* put into Donaghadee in Ireland to acquire supplies for the Atlantic crossing, some of the prisoners had recovered their spirit. The ninety-six surviving prisoners were unloaded from *William* and barricaded in two large barns. But breaking out of a barn was scarcely a problem for a Highlander and soon the Magistrates of Donaghadee, believing that the prisoners were all convicted thieves, issued warrants for their recapture. It would have been easy to find such a large number of Gaelic-speaking Scots in such a small area, and the fugitives were rounded up by force. It was said that the master of *William* was particularly brutal to those who resisted. But the Hebrideans had not been quiet; they had broadcast their story to everybody who would listen.

From hunting the Hebrideans, the Donaghadee authorities began to help them. An official enquiry was instigated, and when it became known that the prisoners were innocent victims rather than convicted felons, they were released. Some returned to the Isles, but not surprisingly most decided to remain in Ireland, where they found friendship and employment. With the threat of arrest, Norman MacLeod and the brutal Master of *William* disappeared abroad, hunted men.

It would make a tidy ending to state that Sir Alexander MacDonald and MacLeod of Harris were also prosecuted, but this did not happen. It appears that they completely escaped, but there is a suspicion that the threat of prosecution was suspended, like the Sword of Damocles, above their head. Both were sympathisers of the Jacobite cause, and both could call out a sizeable array of fighting men, yet when Charles Edward Stuart landed in Scotland, six years later, he found no support from either man. It has been suggested that Duncan

Forbes of Culloden, Lord High Advocate of Scotland, promised the two chiefs that he would take no action against them if they did not rise for Charlie.

Duncan Forbes was a cunning man, wise in the way of the world. He would have known that a few hundred claymores, and the possibly infectious example set by the Skye chiefs, could have altered the course of any Jacobite rising. If the '45 had been a success, the direction of British and possibly of European and even world history might have been altered. The sordid affair of *William* might have been a vital hinge in history.

SECTION III
THE PLACES

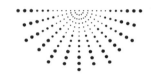

This is the shortest section in the book because, quite frankly, I had to create somewhere to place these stories. They did not seem to fit in anywhere, so here they are. The first, the Claiming of Rona, is set at the extreme north west of Scotland on a tiny scrap of an island. I was there once, landing on the bleak coast in a thick smirr of mist and wondered how people could ever live on such a forbidding place. The next morning, the sun broke through, the sea was calm, and I wondered how people could ever bear to leave such an enchanting place for the noise and confusion of the mainland. But that's a Scottish island for you.

Other stories here cover the varied fishing and

marine life of the Firth of Tay, and the story of the Bell Rock Lighthouse.

THE CLAIMING OF RONA

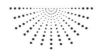

If St Kilda is the most remote of Scotland's West Coast islands, and the Flannan Islands are the most mysterious, Rona can claim to be both remote and mysterious. Lying North West of Cape Wrath, and north of the Butt of Lewis, Rona was inhabited by monks in the Dark Ages, sheep farmers in mediaeval times and was the site of aircraft crashes during Hitler's War. It is an almost insignificant scrap of nowhere, surrounded by some of the most turbulent waters in the world and is continually scoured by a wind that can howl straight down from the Arctic. Rona is a place so dominated by the sea that it was known as *Ronaidh an T'haf*, Rona of the Ocean.

Yet for all its inaccessibility and lack of apparent charms, legend claims that this island was disputed between two rival clans. As usual in Scotland, there are various versions of the story, but all seem to have some aspects in common. The story relates that two rival clans wanted Rona; Clan Mackay from Reay in Sutherland, and Clan MacLeod, or possibly Clan Morrison from Ness at the tip of Lewis. It was agreed that both clans should launch a boat from a point supposedly equidistant from Rona, and the first to light a peat fire on Rona should hold the island. However, while one version of the story states that a 6-oared boat was used, another lengthens the boat to a galley of sixteen oars. This story shall take the Ness Morrisons as the Lewis team, and use the 16-oared galley.

While the Mackay boat left from Cape Wrath at the extreme tip of Sutherland, the Morrison's boat left from Ness and both pulled mightily for Rona. All the men were straining at the long, slim oars as the galleys sped onward with a delicate feather of spray hissing upward from their bow and the steersman calling the time. As the island rose from the horizon, and the two boats came in easy sight of each other, it could be seen that the mainland boat was in front. Not by much, but enough for them to land first. The Morrisons redoubled their efforts, hauling back on the oars, but the Mackays were pulling just as hard, and the distance between the long galleys did not diminish.

'Pull lads!' One of the Morrisons shouted 'and

PIRATES AND PICKLED HEADS

don't mind me!' He had a fire already kindled in the boat and was about to throw it onto the island, when an arrow flew from the Mackay boat, trailing smoke behind it as it carried a flaming peat to Rona. It seemed that the Mackays had won, but the same Morrison who had intended to throw the peat hauled out his dirk, hacked off his hand, or perhaps his little finger and fired that onto the island. Now both sides had staked their claim to the island, but the Morrisons' claim was the stronger, for they had claimed in blood.

Another of the versions of the story claims that the race ended in a battle on the island, during which every man from the mainland was slaughtered. But whatever the details, there is no dispute that from the date of the race, the people of Lewis, and in particular the people from Ness, owned the island of Rona. Separated from the rest of Scotland by an often-stormy sea, it is no wonder that the people of Rona could be conservative in some of their ideas. Martin Martin, the late seventeenth-century writer and traveller related that when the Minister of Barvas, Daniel Morrison, visited Rona, which was in his parish, he was greeted courteously.

'God save you pilgrim' the Rona spokesman said, 'you are heartily welcome here, for we have had repeated apparitions of your person among us, and we heartily congratulate your arrival in our remote country.' As if this reference to second sight was not enough, the men of Rona began to walk sunwise, around the Minister, which was a sign of respect, but very pagan.

Martin said that the Minister was annoyed and ordered the Rona men to stop such heathenish practises.

Other visitors to the island were more unfriendly, with passing seamen occasionally coming ashore to steal the sheep that grazed on Rona's pasture. On one notable occasion in the middle of the eighteenth century, a party of sailors landed, and one took a fancy to an island woman. When his advances were rebuffed, he became insistent, but the women of Rona were a hardy bunch, and she disentangled herself and knocked the sailor down. Rising to his feet, he tried again, so she lifted him bodily and threw him to the ground. Probably hurt more in pride than in person, the sailor stood up and struck back, so the woman's brother came to her aid. Naturally, the other seamen joined in, and within minutes there was a widespread melee.

Eighteenth-century seamen were a tough bunch, but the people of Rona lived all their lives out of doors; their work was physical, and they were fighting to defend one of their own. When one of the sailors was killed, the remainder ran back to their ship, but even though they had won, the men of Rona had no desire to pursue their victory. When unknown seamen visited after that, they hid their women to ensure there was no further trouble.

Perhaps because it is so remote, Rona has been the subject of legend. During the Second World War, there was a strange story circulating about the island. According to one version of the story, the armed trawler, *Preston North End*, was on patrol to the north of Scotland when she had to land a party on the island. Few people get the chance to land on a genuine deserted island, so the sailors explored a little, and came across the body of a dead man. They were surprised to see that he was a German Naval officer, fully dressed in his Number One uniform, complete with peaked hat, and he was sitting upright against a wall. When the seamen searched him, they found neither papers nor identity discs; he was a mystery man. Of course, there was speculation; was he a spy planted to watch the movement of British shipping? Or was the last survivor of a sunken U-boat? It seemed to be yet another mystery of the islands.

The story, however, is apocryphal. There was no body of a uniformed German naval officer. The reality is somewhat different.

In April 1941, the Battle of the Atlantic was at its height. Convoys collected in the sea lochs of western Scotland to sail to Canada and the United States, the northern seas were dangerous with

German warships, and the Royal Navy was guarding the shipping lanes of the free world. During all this, Wing Commander J. Wallis took a Whitley aircraft of 612 Squadron on a flight from Wick, in Caithness. The plane was testing secret equipment, perhaps related to the still-developing radar, or maybe it was a version of Asdic. Either way, the equipment was carried beneath each wing and made the Whitley awkward to fly.

When Wing Commander Wallis reached Rona, he turned back, but as he did, an oil pump in the port engine fractured. With one engine out of action, and the equipment unbalancing the aircraft, Wallis had to make a quick decision. Should he attempt to fly back on one engine, or should he land on Rona? If he tried to return and ditched in the sea, both the aircraft and the equipment would be lost, which at a time that Britain was struggling alone against half of Europe may have had disastrous consequences. Wallis checked the weather; if the wind was westerly, he might have a chance, but it came from the east, blowing against him, and already he was losing height. The sea beneath was high and rough, with the wind flicking white spray from the crest of evil green rollers; it would be unpleasant to ditch in that.

Circling around the tiny scrap of island, Wallis used the wind to reduce his airspeed as he came in from the west. Before he landed, he radioed for help and eased the Whitley to the best possible landing in the circumstances. It took only four hours for a rescue launch to arrive from Thurso, and immediately preparations began to salvage the wrecked aircraft and its precious equipment. It was now that the armed trawler, *Preston North End*, landed a party and found the body of a man. Rather than the uniform of a German Naval Officer, the man wore only rags, and he appeared to have been sheltering in a house when he died. There was a story here, but it was poignant rather than mysterious.

Probably nobody will ever know the identity of the body found on Rona, but in 1941 many ships were being murdered at sea. Some men died at once, others were rescued, but some drifted on lifeboats, rafts, and on scraps of equipment for days. Presumably, one man, the survivor of a torpedoed ship, drifted to Rona. He may have called for help; he may have searched for life on this deserted island. There is no telling his anguish when he realised he was alone, and no nearer rescue than he had been at sea. At length, he would have crawled to the shelter of one of the ruined houses where the people of Rona had lived, and died there, perhaps still hoping for succour. Rona is an eternally mysterious place, and this lone body only adds to the loneliness of the wind-scoured island.

From the eternal loneliness of Rona, it is a long step to the bustling Firth of Tay, and the industry and marine life of the nineteenth century, but such a contrast is part of the fascination of maritime Scotland.

SPRATS, STAKE NETS, AND SMUGGLERS

While people automatically associate Aberdeen with fishing, and Edinburgh had an excellent fleet of trawlers and drifters at Granton, Dundee's past as a fishing port is virtually unknown. Yet at one time Dundee had the third largest trawling fleet in Scotland, while boats from Broughty Ferry hunted for herring up and down the coast of Britain.

In the nineteenth century, the Tay was a far busier waterway than it is now. As well as ships carrying flax from the Baltic and raw jute from India, there were whalers and ferries, colliers and coasters, brigs and steamers, and the great three-masted vessels of the Dundee Clipper Line. These vessels would nose carefully past the sandbanks at the entrance of the Tay, some gratefully accepting the services of a Tay Pilot, who, in the early years of the century would be a fisherman from Broughty or Arbroath, before berthing at Dundee. Most likely the Master and crew would be far too busy to notice the other life of the Firth, but if any naturalist of the twenty-first century could be transported back, he or she would be in raptures at the wildlife on display.

Contemporary accounts speak of 'flocks' of seals that occupied every sandbank from the Sands of Tay to Flisk, while pods of grampus and porpoise, hundreds strong, hunted the waters. There were so many seals that at the beginning of the nineteenth century the brothers Alexander and Thomas Boiter were employed full time in hunting them down. They lived in a hut on the outskirts of Dundee and sailed a small boat to reach the sandbanks where the seals lived.

The grampuses appeared in the Firth from July to September, moving upstream with the flow of the tide and withdrawing with the ebb, while the porpoise season was April to August. All three creatures were in the river for one purpose; they were hunting the salmon, 'like a pack of hounds' as Mr Stuart, the shepherd of Balmerino, stated. The turn of the eighteenth and nineteenth century was an unfortunate time to be a Tay salmon, for it was then that men also began to intensify their hunting techniques.

Of course, people had fished for salmon for centuries. Scotland had exported salmon as far as the Mediterranean in the fifteenth century, and salmon had been a staple food for servants for years. However, in the 1790s fishermen from the Solway began to work in the Tay. Solway fishermen employed a unique technique of spreading nets around tidal pools so that salmon were trapped when the tide receded. With the Firth of Tay tidal, the Solway men adapted their methods and invented the stake net. These nets extended into the tidal current of the river, where the salmon swam and guided the fish into a fish trap, where they could be harvested.

At the beginning of the nineteenth century, virtually every sandbank of the Tay had such a net, and the catch of salmon increased tremendously. However, the landowners of the Upper Tay protested that so many fish were being captured in the Firth that they were losing money. Being landowners, they had political clout and persuaded the House of Commons to ban stake nets in the Firth. There was a public enquiry, during which the views of fishermen on both sides of the divide were heard, but the ban was retained, with stake nets only being allowed along the coast.

The dispute between estuarial and inland salmon fishermen was only one of many that disturbed the tidal waters of the Tay. Another argument simmered between the herring fishermen of Broughty Ferry and the sprat fishermen of Newburgh and the Carse of Gowrie. The sprat fishing boats sailed in winter, with most of their catch either being sold as manure or sent to the London market, although there was a brief period of prosperity when the Norwegian sprat fishery failed, and Tay sprats were exported. Sprats were also important during the dark years of the First World War when the U-boats sunk so many British ships that there was only two weeks supply of food in the country.

In theory, the sprat men were only permitted to fish upstream of Dundee, but they seem to have strayed from time to time. The Fishery Officer at Montrose, whose territory included Dundee, had to contend with a string of complaints from the Broughty herring fishermen that sprat men were invading their territory. As long as the Newburgh men only caught sprats, there was no major problem, but their bag nets tended to scoop up everything, including young salmon.

The men of the Ferry, however, were no angels themselves. Sometimes Customs Officers from Dundee chased over the wide sands of Broughty to catch suspected smugglers. It was believed that Broughty fishermen helped returning whaling ships to unload some of their duty-free spirits and tobacco before they berthed in Dundee. On the

PIRATES AND PICKLED HEADS

evening of Saturday 21st October 1854 George Murray, the Acting Tidesman at Broughty Ferry chased over the sands to watch a fishing boat with the historic name of *Fall* sail toward the whaling ship Heroine as she returned from the Arctic. The Customs men waited until the fishing boat, owned by Alexander Gall, returned to the jetty when they rummaged her. Finding six pounds of concealed tobacco, they seized the boat. Alexander Gall protested that, although he owned the boat, it had been taken without his knowledge and he had nothing to do with any smuggling. Strangely, the customs men agreed and returned the boat. One man, named Lorimer, was convicted of the smuggling offence, and was fined £3 10/-.

A different case occurred in February 1878 when SS *Arctic*, another whaler, outward bound for the Davis Strait, stopped temporarily at Broughty Ferry. A steam lighter, owned by Mr Adams, brother of the Master of *Arctic*, put out from the pier and returned with a collection of passengers from the ship. Mr Bell, one of the minor Custom officials, became quite excited and immediately forbade any of the passengers to land until they had been searched for contraband goods.

The passengers of the lighter were astonished. As well as the master's brother, Mr Stephen, shipbuilder and the owner of *Arctic* was present, together with Mr Hume, a merchant and other of his friends. There were also several ladies. According to Mr Bell, the passengers became: 'greatly excited, shoving me about and shouting that I had nothing to do with them.' The passengers stated that Mr Bell had no authority over gentlemen and certainly could not search anybody without his superior, but when the passengers attempted to step ashore, he 'seized one…by the throat collar and another by the coat.' Mr Bell claimed that he was pushed against one of the passengers, felt a bundle in his pocket and asked if it was tobacco, after which one of Mr Bell's men grabbed hold of him.

While the ladies fled to a cab, the gentlemen 'assembled in the Customs watch-house at Broughty Pier.' It seems that Bell asked them individually if they had contraband goods, then released them. Although it appears that Mr Bell was only performing his duty in searching possible smugglers, he had to issue an apology. In the late nineteenth century, gentlemen and, perhaps especially ladies, thought they were somehow more important than fishermen and believed officials should treat them differently. There was never any suggestion that the Customs men impounded the steam lighter.

The Broughty Ferry fishermen seem to have been quite an independent lot. The fishing industry peaked towards the end of the nineteenth century, when the tremendous lug-sailed Fifies, with their near vertical stems and sterns, sailed into the Tay and beyond. The fishermen berthed their boats on the beach as much as in the new harbour, for the beach was free, and handy for painting and simple repairs.

Women played a significant part in the fishing industry. As well as gathering bait from the extensive mussel beds that were situated off Broughty, they also ran the family finances and baited the lines. Women could also own fishing boats. In 1868 the Fishery Act ordered that all fishing boats had to be registered and the size and owner recorded. The Register of Fishing Boats is held in Dundee Archives, and the first entry of the first volume deals with the first-class fishing vessel *Matilda* of Broughty Ferry, a half decked lugger with two masts had a crew of eight men. She was seventeen tons in weight, over forty-two feet long and a Mrs Barbara Ferrier or Bell owned her.

In 1883 Barbara Bell also owned the four-ton *John* and *Davids* while Elizabeth Gowans of Broughty owned a twenty-eight ton, fully decked boat. The Master was John Anderson Mrs Thomas Webster, also of Broughty Ferry owned two boats, the first class, thirty-ton *Isabella*, skippered by Robert Webster, who was presumably her husband, and the two-ton *David*, skippered by David Webster, who may have been her son.

Despite the influence of the women that

Victorians portrayed as 'Angels of the House', there was also a history of disputes between the Broughty herring fishermen and the Tay Salmon Fishing Company, which was based much further up the river. The Company claimed that Broughty fishermen were illegally catching salmon in their nets, and even boarded the Broughty boats from time to time. Unfortunately for the reputation of Broughty Ferry, there appears to have been some basis for the accusations. There was even a case when the local policeman hawked poached salmon through the streets of the town.

Dundee however, hoped for a larger slice of the fishing industry. Steam trawlers and drifters had transformed the industry, with the steam tug *Toiler* starting a process that saw Aberdeen grow into the largest fishing port in Scotland. Dundee watched with envy but planned a fish dock with railway access, cheap coal, and cheap ice to pack the catch. At the beginning of the twentieth century, Dundee sent delegations to the major trawler and drifter companies in an attempt to entice them away from Aberdeen.

Unfortunately, there was only limited success. While Aberdeen had over two hundred trawlers, Dundee barely scraped into double figures. However, some of these vessels had an exciting time. With the Dundee trawlers mainly fishing off the East Coast, U-boats attacked some in the First

World War and aircraft in the Second. Others were convicted of illegal fishing, but overall, they helped provide fish for the hundreds of fish and chip shops in Dundee. It is a shame that these vessels never quite succeeded in becoming part of Dundee's folklore, for they were interesting, hard-working boats.

Today the Firth of Tay is free of sprat boats, although the salmon still swim upriver and seals bask on the sandbank beneath the Tay Bridge. Disputes about stake nets have been forgotten, and no Customs men are watching from the sands of Broughty as the tide slowly creeps in.

Further up the storied east coast, history clings to every curve and cove, with a surge of legend and tales around Arbroath, that most evocative of ports.

A BELL, A ROVER, AND A NORTH SEA GRAVEYARD

When the wind comes from the southeast and the long grey rollers explode on the sea wall of Arbroath, legend speaks of a bell that can be heard, tolling sombrely from the sea. It is said to be most audible within the confines of the old shore station of the lighthouse, now known as the Signal Tower Museum. Perhaps there is a sound, transmitted under the sea by the constant movement of waves against the rocky coast of Angus, but the story of the bell persists, supported by an ancient tale of piracy, greed, and ironic misfortune.

Arbroath was a religious town, with an abbey that was one of the most important in Scotland. Founded by King William the Lion in 1178, it was home to the Brecbennoth of St Columba but is probably bettered remembered as the place where the Declaration of Independence was signed in 1320. In common with other religious foundations, Arbroath Abbey was a centre of trade, with supply ships using the harbour that lies within chanting distance of the rose-walled building that dominated the town. Also in common with other religious institutions, Arbroath Abbey is said to have guided travellers away from danger. Where the Border Abbeys used lanterns to indicate the safest path across the moorland and wastes of the south, Arbroath used a bell to warn seafarers away from the vicious Inchcape Rock.

One hundred feet in width, the Inchcape Rock lies about twelve miles east of Arbroath and stretches for about 2000 feet of wave flogged nightmare. Lying across the busy shipping route to the Forth and Tay, menacing the coast of Angus, this rock would be dangerous enough if it was visible. It was far more dangerous because, often, it was not. At the highest spring tide, sixteen feet of water covers the Inchcape rock, but at low tide, it protrudes four feet above the sea. In between these extremes, there is neither enough water to cover it in safety nor enough land for it to be always visible. In those conditions, the Inchcape Rock became the graveyard of the North Sea.

Add the danger of treacherous weather to the menace of a hidden reef and the Inchcape's reputation is not hard to understand. A gale may be defined as a wind that reaches thirty-eight miles per hour for at least an hour. In the early 1960s, a study of the Bell Rock found it has an average of 255 hours of gales a year. On land a storm can be a nuisance; trees may be uprooted, roofs can be damaged. At sea, the combination of wind and waterpower can be terrifying. When the Bell Rock lighthouse was being built in the century, large rocks were frequently torn from the seabed and thrown onto the Inchcape Rock. These boulders could weigh over two tons each. Spray often spatters to a height of 120 feet, or more, upon the structure of the lighthouse.

Given these facts, it was no wonder that the monks of Arbroath decided to help seafarers avoid this terrible place. It is unfortunate that so many historic documents have disappeared from Scotland through warfare, religious upheaval, and general waste, and even folklore is declining, as people prefer electronically generated media to the collective memories of their ancestors. However, folklore is strong on the monk's part in marking the Inchcape Rock.

Rather than a light, which would have required a virtually permanent presence on Inchcape, Abbot John Gedy, who in 1394 had built Arbroath's first harbour, fixed a bell in such a manner that the movement of the sea caused it to ring a warning to

PIRATES AND PICKLED HEADS

passing ships. Robert Stevenson proposed such a device on the North Carr centuries later. It is possible that the bell was fastened to a broad-based post, secured to the rock with wickerwork gabions filled with stones. If that sounds a problematic task, spend some time to consider the great abbeys of the period. Abbey building, like castle building, flourished from the twelfth century as pilgrims and Crusaders learned new construction techniques from the skilled engineers of the Middle East. After building Arbroath Abbey, fixing a post to a rock, and placing a bell on top would be little more than an exciting challenge. No doubt the bell came adrift from time to time, but Angus was an area of seafarers, a twenty-four-mile return trip would hardly be noticed.

However, not only peaceful traders and fishermen used the sea. The Middle Ages were notorious for piracy, and one such haunted the area around Angus. It is here that history completely fails us, and folklore remains as a guide. It was Robert Southey who wrote the famous poem Ralph the Rover, but it is based on a far earlier tradition. Ralph the Rover was a local pirate and wrecker who made his living from looting the ships that were wrecked on the Inchcape Rock. He was annoyed when the monks placed their bell there, for the absence of shipwrecks lost him his source of income. According to Southey, Ralph removed the bell and sailed away to await the next batch of wrecks. Unfortunately for him, about a year later the Rover returned to the rock, running aground on the Inchcape that no longer held the warning bell.

> Sir Ralph the Rover tore his
>   hair;
> He curst himself in his despair.

Although the rock may be officially known as Inchcape, few people call it other than the Bell Rock. It seems that the monks did not replace their bell, but there is another tradition that they lit up the Catherine window of the abbey as a beacon to mariners. Seen from the sea, the rose-stoned magnificent abbey would be eye-catching, and the Round O became a noted mark for both fishermen and traders coming to the burgh, whose inhabitants became known as Red Lighties.

Yet for all the efforts of the monks, the Inchcape Rock remained a horrendous hazard to shipping. Vessel after vessel came to grief on the half-hidden reef, and ships were known to alter their route, so they did not have to pass the rock. Scotland had long had a thriving trade with Northern Europe, but by the late eighteenth century, the North Sea was a highway as ships passed from Scotland to Europe and carried goods coastwise from every port in Britain. The turning of the eighteenth to the nineteenth century saw a series of storms that highlighted the danger of the unmarked Inchcape Rock.

December 1799 saw one of those storms that mariners reminisced over and no wonder. The storm seems to have started on the second of the month and lasted for three terrible days. Perhaps as many as seventy vessels were wrecked on the East Coast of Scotland, with five driven ashore at Arbroath alone, and the same story emerged from the lips of those seamen who survived. 'We would have run for the shelter of the Forth,' they said, 'but for fear of piling onto the Bell Rock.' The fear was well founded, for two of the vessels that did run for the Forth were smashed to pieces on the greasy fangs of the rock.

There was talk of erecting a lighthouse on the rock after that nightmare episode, but it was not until two years after the wreck of the 64-gun battleship HMS *York* in January 1804 that permission was given to begin the work. Robert Stevenson was the engineer chosen, and at first, it must have seemed a next to impossible task. *Comet*, the world's first commercially successful steam-powered boat, had not yet been launched in the Clyde, so Stevenson had to rely on the expertise of local seamen to carry all the equipment, all the material and the entire workforce out to the rock. He could only work when the tide allowed access onto the rock, and only then if the weather was calm, and he had to ensure that one day's work was not ruined by the storms of the next. Even on the best days, only five hours of work could be done before the tide swooped back, and when the gales came howling in, the building site became a maelstrom of raging water.

The stone was carried from Aberdeen, from Craigleith in Edinburgh, and from Mylnefield near Dundee, coastwise to Arbroath. Twenty-eight builders, headed by Robert Stevenson, lived in what was termed 'the barracks'; a precarious looking hut erected on legs of wood on the rock itself. There is no denying the skill of the engineer and his men, and no denying their bravery either, but there were compensations, as these workmen were all issued with Protections that ensured they could not be pressed into the Navy. The barracks must have been a terrifying home when the wind was up, and waves battered against the wooden legs of their home. Work was completed in 1811, and the bright warning beam of the lighthouse gleamed on the site of the Rover's demise. When a North Sea haar ghosted grey across the water, the sonorous beat of a more modern bell than that of the monks warned shipping that they were in danger.

Since that day there has never been a wreck on the rock when the light was lit, but on the occasions

PIRATES AND PICKLED HEADS

when there was no light, the Bell Rock again became a danger. During the First World War, a combination of German U-boats and minefields made the North Sea as hazardous as it had ever been. Many Scottish lighthouses were blacked out for security purposes, being lit only when vessels of the Royal Navy were known to be passing. Because of bad weather, the keepers had not been warned of the passage of a naval vessel in late October 1915, and the Rock claimed another major victim.

HMS *Argyll* had been built on the Clyde; an 11,000-ton armoured cruiser capable of taking on anything less than a battlecruiser. Before the war, *Argyll* had been part of the Atlantic fleet and had escorted King George V in his trip to India for the Delhi Durbar, possibly because she was one of the first ships to carry wireless. Argyll was 450 feet long, with four 7.5-inch, and six 6-inch guns, and she was commanded by Captain James Tancred. She was proceeding at her full speed of some twenty-two knots, zigzagging to confuse enemy submarines while still navigating around minefields, both enemy and friendly, when she piled up on the Bell Rock. Although it was half past four on a bitter October morning, Captain Tancred immediately assessed the damage. He organised a boom to keep off the worst of the weather, and sent a line to the lighthouse keepers, attached to a hawser.

There were 655 men on board, and a full-scale rescue mission began at once. By half past six two destroyers had powered from Rosyth and crammed about 400 of the crew aboard. Tancred ordered others into the ship's boats, while one of the ubiquitous requisitioned trawlers, *Jackal*, rescued more.

With the crew rescued, an inspection of the wreck revealed that she could not be salvaged, but much valuable equipment was rescued. For a while, the Bell Rock resembled a giant breaker's yard, with tugs and lighters carrying off the ranger finder, searchlights, the six-inch guns, and everything else that they could find. If the ghost of Ralph, the one-time wrecker, was present, he must have approved of all this activity on his rock.

Argyll was not the last casualty on the rock, although she was probably the most valuable. In December 1939, when the lighthouse had once again donned its wartime blackout, the steam trawler *Quixotic* slammed aground directly beneath the lighthouse. The keepers let down ropes, but these were too short, so the crew set their bedding alight to attract attention, and the Broughty Ferry lifeboat rescued all nine men.

There is an excellent display on the Bell Rock lighthouse in the Signal Tower Museum in Arbroath, itself once the home station for the keepers and their families. Artefacts from the light are here, with one of the great bells that sounded through the mist and may have saved thousands of lives. The Bell Rock Lighthouse remains the oldest sea-washed lighthouse in the world.

On a clear day, it is possible to see the slender stack of the Bell Rock Lighthouse rising from the sea, and despite the gales, there are days like that along the Angus coast. It is better on a still night when the sea hushes quietly on the long beaches south of Arbroath, and the oystercatchers pipe their way across the surf, to look seaward. The light is always there, familiar, reassuring, a memorial to the seamen who never did come home as much as to the monks who tried their best to make the seas a safer place. And perhaps, if the wind is in the right quarter, it may be possible to hear, beneath the constant shush of the sea, the faint tolling of a bell.

SECTION IV
THE PIRATES

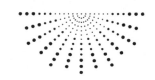

Most people have heard about pirates, with the romantic image being that created by the Edinburgh author Robert Louis Stevenson in *Treasure Island*, a one-legged man from the English West Country, with a tricorne hat and a parrot. Although the figure of Long John Silver might sit comfortably in the early eighteenth-century Caribbean, the facts of piracy are much more widespread and stretch longer into history. As a maritime nation, Scotland had her quota of pirates, equally as unpleasant and dangerous as those from any other country. One of the most interesting was even a belted earl.

HIGHLAND GALLEYS AND A PIRATE EARL

While Scotland's Dark Ages were highlighted by the epic voyages of intrepid Celtic monks and scarred by the raids of the Vikings, the Middle Ages were also dangerous days for the maritime traveller. The seas of northern Europe were well known, and trading vessels followed recognised routes to ports that were already expanding into cities. Each voyage was an adventure, with the natural hazards of the sea always augmented by the possibility of every strange sail being a pirate. No sea was safe, and often the coastal communities were as much threatened in the thirteenth century as they had been in the ninth. Nonetheless, lone ships were most at risk. For instance, Richard de Alverstone, a merchant from Scotland's then premier port of

Berwick, had his vessel pirated in 1229. At a time when relations with England had not yet deteriorated by incessant war, he was able to claw back some of his possessions when he recognised woolpacks at Sandwich as part of his cargo.

Not only the reiving spirit of the Norseman had been retained, but often Viking blood ran in the veins of men who would scorn any thought of Thor. Hebridean piracy predated the Norse, for Saint Columba stumbled across the pirate Loan of the Cenel Gabrain ravaging the home of a friend and cursed him with a venom that would have been surprising in any other saint. Sometimes vast fleets of pirate vessels slipped out of Scottish ports to wreak havoc on unsuspecting communities. Such an event occurred in 1212 when Thomas of Galloway teamed up with the grandson of Somerled to take seventy galleys across the narrow seas to Ireland. The combined Galwegian and Hebridean fleet descended on Inishowen and Derry to spread some very unromantic terror.

Such raids were not uncommon during the mediaeval period as island chieftains flexed their muscles or attempted to curb the energy of their young warriors. In 1258, with Scotland officially at peace with all her neighbours, it was Dugald, son of Ruairi, Lord of Garmoran, who called up all his followers to board their galleys. Steering south, Dugald led the pride of the Hebrides to the western shores of Ireland. Whatever other damage they did, the galley fleet certainly came across an Anglo-Irish merchant ship, which they plundered of 'wine, copper, cloth, and iron.' Naturally enraged, Jordan de Exeter, the Englishman who claimed to be Sheriff of Connacht, whistled up his own fleet and set off in pursuit of the Hebrideans.

It is unfortunate that there are few details, but there was a battle in which Dugald and his galleys were victorious. Sheriff Jordan de Exeter was defeated and killed, and the Hebrideans returned home with much plunder. Only a few years later there was real war in the land as Norseman and Scot clashed for ownership of the islands claimed by the Gael. By the end of the century that war paled with the longer, bloodier war between Scot and Englishman, with the independence of Scotland the prize.

Scots and English clashed at sea as well as on land. Piracy was endemic as freebooters used war as an excuse to enrich themselves, and privateers, merchant vessels licensed to loot the enemy in the name of their respective kings, roamed freely along all the coasts of Scotland, Ireland, Wales, and England. Despite their preponderance of population, the English did not find the Scots an easy enemy. While the guerrilla forces of Bruce, Douglas, and Wallace cut invaders to bloody shreds, Scots ships hunted off the coasts of England.

Based in the ports of France, Scottish privateers ravaged shipping from the English south coast ports. In 1314 Scots ships were so active along the English East Coast that English vessels had to sail in convoy. After a temporary peace with the Treaty of Edinburgh, hostilities resumed, and the sea became a nightmare of plundered ships and terrified coastal communities.

While English pirates targeted the firths of Forth and Tay, Scottish vessels retaliated by raiding towns along the coast of East Anglia. In April 1335, the Scots privateer vessel John of St Agatha made her name by sinking the Southampton vessel *Lecheward*, while other Scottish ships savaged the coast and shipping of the Channel Islands. Forced to fortify Lindisfarne and the Inner Farne Islands, the English continued their own aggressive campaign against Scottish shipping with a combination of royal warships, licensed privateers, and sheer piracy. They did not only target Scottish shipping, but also vessels of the Flemings, allies of the Scots. One of the most notable English successes was their capture of the Flemish *Pelarym*. No doubt pleased with the £2000 of cargo, the English pirates murdered all the Scots on board, including pilgrims and women.

Despite all these events, very few personalities have been recorded. Each incident was traumatic to the people involved, but history has drawn a shaded veil over motive and character. It is maddeningly frustrating to work with only hints and scarce recordings of events. However, the early fifteenth century saw the emergence of a more detailed personality, a North Sea pirate who was also a belted earl.

The Wolf of Badenoch is one of the more flamboyant figures of the late fourteenth century. He was a wild outlaw who spread fear from his fortress on Lochindorb, and if his best-remembered exploit was to burn Elgin Cathedral, that was only one of a catalogue of crimes that put him in the forefront of Scottish bad-men. However colourful his life, he still had time to spawn a son, whose life was every bit as eventful, and possibly as unlawful.

If Alexander Stewart started life as the illegitimate son of a wolfish father, he ended as one of Scotland's premier nobleman and holder of the highest maritime position in the nation. There can be few better instances of local boy made good, and if it is considered that he made his way by piracy, abduction, and battle, the story becomes even more intriguing. Much of the life of Alexander Stewart appears to have been lived aggressively, but he thrived in a period when maritime laws were vague, and every sea voyage was an adventure. As a small country bordering England, that most nautical of nations whose seamen were a byword for piracy, Scottish mariners tended to develop a truculence all of their own. So it is hardly surprising that when the North Sea was alive with pirates, Scottish ports and Scottish seamen played their part.

When the Plantagenet kings of England sent their fleets to blockade Scottish ports, daring captains slipped past the English ships with vital supplies. German vessels, in particular, seemed to have continued trading with Scotland so that in 1310 nine Germans were arrested in Boston for trading with Dundee. This European alliance was in full blossom two years later when German vessels sailed into Aberdeen to sell the goods they had liberated from English shipping. German fighters also helped the Scots remove the occupying English from that same port, so Aberdeen was very much part of the North Sea network. Alexander Stewart grew up with Aberdeen as a background to the unlawful deeds of his father.

The son of a fighting father, Alexander Stewart was cursed by being young, aggressive, and vigorous at a time when Scotland was officially at peace. France and England were also at peace, but national law did not extend far beyond the nautical horizon, and in 1402 the Duke of Orleans had hired David Lindsay, Earl of Crawford and Admiral of Scotland, to lead a Scottish fleet to attack English shipping. Young Alexander may have heard of

Crawford's exploits, but at the time he was busy securing himself a wife.

A few years earlier Isabella Douglas had become heir to the Earldom of Mar, which bordered Badenoch. She promptly married Sir Malcolm Drummond, but in 1402 a band of anonymous predators captured Sir Malcolm and popped him in prison, where he died. Perhaps Alexander Stewart had been implicated in Sir Malcolm's demise, maybe not, but he certainly made full use of it. As the son of the Wolf of Badenoch, Alexander whistled up a band of caterans from Clan Chattan country, led them over the tangled hills to Kildrummie Castle and abducted Isabella. It was not uncommon for Highlandmen to kidnap Lowland women as a wife, but unusual for a Countess to be the victim. However, Alexander put a gloss of legality to the act, for he placed Isabella at the gates of her own Kildrummie, presented her with the keys and charter of the castle and told her she was free to do with them as she willed.

There might have been some persuasion involved, but it is always possible that the Countess actually liked this wild young man, but as she held the keys, she told whoever was gathered that she chose him as her husband. So Alexander Stewart became a respectable married man and the Earl of Mar, one of the oldest and most established earldoms in Europe. This sudden descent into respectability did not in the least alter the new Earl's natural disposition to criminal violence, but many Scottish youths were disorderly, and some even grew out of it. Perhaps time would soothe the savagery of Alexander Stewart.

In 1405, with the honeymoon over and his belt of earldom hanging comfortably from his hips, Mar commanded a Scottish flotilla that blockaded the port of Berwick. In as much as Berwick was a Scottish town in English occupation, his actions were justified, but his probing south to menace shipping sailing into Newcastle was pure aggression. Used to tales about predatory English mariners such as Drake and Hawkins, it is perhaps sobering to realise that Scottish seamen could be just as piratical and that English ports were as vulnerable as any other in Europe. But Mar did not limit his attacks only to English targets.

It was around 1406 that the Earl of Mar met Provost Robert Davidson of Aberdeen at a tavern in that city's Ship Row. By then Mar was an experienced mariner, as well as a practised drinker who had rocked the Tin Plate Inn in Paris while he entertained friends and colleagues in a weeks-long binge of drinking feasting and dancing. Nobody will ever know what Mar and Provost Davidson discussed as they piled the empties beneath the table, but if it was business, it meant trouble for some poor mariner. It is possible that Mar was persuading Davidson to join him in some scheme that was at best only marginally lawful. As an innkeeper, customs inspector, and major wine merchant, Davidson was fully aware of shipping movements in the North Sea. Given the proven persuasive powers of the Earl of Mar, it is equally possible that he was pumping Davidson for information.

Whatever the topic of conversation, by 1408 the maritime towns of the Low Countries were buzzing with indignation. Scottish mariners, they claimed, were so bored with the English peace that they were infesting the North Sea and attacking any ship they came across.

The townsfolk could quote particulars. There was the case of Nieuwpoort in Flanders when an unknown Scottish vessel attacked a Dutch ship. The Dutch skipper, a man, named Walich, was as stout and honest a merchant as Rotterdam had ever produced, had been overpowered and forced to hand over his goods. Amsterdam goods at that! And there was the Scottish pirate that haunted the estuary of the Zwin in Flanders, not to mention the piratical Scots who had robbed the substantial merchants from Harlem and Gouda. So why was somebody not doing something about it? At that time, nobody was.

Tongues may have wagged, and fingers may have pointed toward the Earl of Mar, but he had a cast iron alibi. In 1407 the Duke of Burgundy had confirmed that Scots traders should continue to enjoy trading privileges in his lands in the Low Countries, and Mar had crossed to help him in a private war. The Earl had commanded the vanguard of his army at the Battle of Othee when it crushed a revolt by the people of Liege. Not even the son of the Wolf could be in two places at once. However having cemented the trade agreement with Scottish swords, Mar returned home and took to the sea in earnest.

The peace with England still held, but Mar sailed south and captured *Thomas and Marie* of London as she voyaged toward Calais. There would be quite a bit of chuckling in Aberdeen when they realised that the cargo of the English vessel belonged to Richard Whittington, Lord Mayor of London, and future pantomime star. Times had turned again for him, and nobody denied that the pirate was the Earl of Mar. What could poor merchants do against a fierce, powerful noble like that?

Not a great deal, individually, but the maritime ports of Northern Europe were quite formidable when they united. Within a year the ports of Browershaven, Flushing and Zierickzel had sent armed ships to scour the seas for Scottish pirates. They would make a brave show too, with their high forecastles and sterncastles packed with men, the sun glittering from steel breastplates and spear points, sheaves of arrows in the fighting tops and perhaps even a small cannon or two. However, before all these arms could be used, the ships had to find the pirates, and even the North Sea was vast compared to the tiny cockleshells that men sailed in the fifteenth century. The Scottish pirates continued their depredations.

First, the Scots took a vessel of Amsterdam. The men on board would see the square sail lift over the horizon, would see the black dot of a lookout on the crosstrees, and would wonder. The strange vessel would close, and then a flag might be hoisted, the heraldic symbols making it evident that the Earl of Mar was back on the high seas. Perhaps the Amsterdam vessel tried to run, but she was a merchantman, deeply laden, with a small crew. The Aberdeen pirate would be faster, would carry a larger crew of wild men, and there could be little contest.

That seems to have been a busy year for the Pirate Earl. While he was being blamed for captures at sea, it was also rumoured that he was the *'bastard d'Escoce qui se appelot conte d'Hembe'*, the illegitimate Scottish knight that fought alongside the Teutonic Knights at the Battle of Tannenberg in 1410. However, when Scottish pirates captured a ship belonging to the immensely powerful Hanseatic League, the major trading organisation of Northern

Europe, it was evident that something had to be done. The Earl of Mar and his fellow pirates had to be curbed, but why had a belted earl turned to seemingly indiscriminate piracy in the first place? Was it out of a sense of devilment? Sheer badness? Or did Mar have some reasonable excuse for his conduct?

Isabella, Countess of Mar, had died, and Alexander Stewart quickly hitched himself to a Lady of Flanders. Very like Stewart's previous wife, this woman owned lands in her native country, but unfortunately, there was a slight snag. The charming lady from Flanders had omitted to mention her first husband, the man to whom she was still married. It is doubtful if the Earl was concerned at the tangled morality, but when his wife's tenants refused to add their rent money to his coffers, he was displeased. If the people of Flanders did not pay him one way, they would have to pay another. It was then that the Earl decided to collect his rent forcibly from Flemish ships.

But either the Earl's geography was faulty, or one ship at sea looked very much like another, for it was his ship that captured a vessel from Danzig, a port that belonged to the powerful Hanseatic League. Perhaps the Earl was a pirate, but he was a reasonably humane man and released the captain and mate of the ship. He was even generous enough to give them a small boat and allow them to row to land. The others of the crew he carried prisoner back to Scotland, where they were employed as labourers on a castle, which may have been Inverness. It is possible that the unfortunate captain was named Claus Bellekow, who was captured in 1412 while sailing from Bergen to Rostock.

Two years earlier Mar had sent Provost Davidson to Harfleur, where he followed his legitimate trade of wine merchant. Unfortunately, the cargo he attempted to sell had been pirated from a Dutch merchant ship. Only the French safe conduct that he held saved him from uncomfortable questions, but the Scots were not so charitable and charged him with piracy. Playing with the big boys had landed the Provost in serious trouble.

Whether or not their reaction related to the same incident, the Hanseatic League were aggrieved at the Scots cavalier treatment of their people and proposed an embargo on Scottish trade. Scotland exported wool, cloth, fish, warriors, imported timber, and grain. Danzig and Stralsund, which had such a large volume of trade that a few incidents of piracy could be ignored, hesitated. So both trade and piracy continued until around 1415 when the Hanseatic ports were closed to Scottish shipping, and Hanseatic ships no longer visited Scotland. There is no doubt that the volume of trade dropped, with Leith seeing its Baltic shipping fall by over 75%. However, Scottish business must have been important to Europe for by 1416 it had recovered, despite the embargo remaining officially in force until 1435.

In the meantime, Mar was not idle. Perhaps he was a villain at sea, but on land, he was, if not a hero, then at least a doughty warrior. In 1411 Donald, Lord of the Isles led his thousands of wild Hebrideans against Aberdeen, and the Earl of Mar commanded the army that barred his path. It would be an oversimplification to say that Scotland was split between Highlander and Lowlander, for Alexander Stewart had a full measure of Gaelic blood in him, and Donald had already defeated the Mackays before his army clashed with Mar. The opposing forces met near Inverurie in a show of hand-to-hand butchery that became known as 'Red' Harlaw from the amount of blood spilt. Perhaps there was no clear victor, but the Islesmen did not descend on Aberdeen, although Provost Davidson was among the six hundred or so dead in Mar's ranks. Dying a hero perhaps saved him from the ignominious end of being hanged as a pirate, but Scottish history is riddled with such anomalies.

Pirate or not, in 1414 the king appointed Mar as Admiral of Scotland, responsible for administering maritime law. The irony of that appointment is hard to beat. The naval war with the Low Countries continued until the early 1420s, but without any real rancour. Seamen expected the odd pirate in the North Sea, but few were as colourful, or as well connected, as the Earl of Mar. Alexander Stewart refused to be tamed by maturity, and in 1431 he again led a Royal army to fight Clan Donald. This time there was no doubt about the outcome as Alastair Carrach attacked in the flank and Donald Balloch landed Islesmen from his galley fleet to defeat the Royal troops. It is good to know that the Earl survived both the battle and the retreat to Kildrummie, where he had once gained a bride and a title.

However, Mar was only one wild man at a time that the sea was as dangerous as the Border hill country between Scotland and England. The sea was seen as a highway, the horizon was inviting, and fortunes were to be made and lost as ship design improved and new lands were discovered.

COGS, CARAVELS, AND PICKLED HEADS

The Middle Ages saw significant improvements in ship design. From the superb open boats of the Norsemen, Northern Europeans turned to the cog, a clinker-built vessel with rounded bow and stern, a broad beam, and clumsy fore and aft castles. This vessel was slow, often unwieldy, and powered by a single mast. In the late fourteenth century, new types of sailing craft appeared on northern seas. First came the hulks, vessels that had a sharper stern and stem, but neither keel nor stern post and could carry large cargoes. Then came the caravel or carvel, a ship that was an adaptation of the Mediterranean craft and lacked the sterncastles that fighting mariners had found so useful.

It was the Portuguese, that essentially maritime

nation that sat on the western edge of the known world, who first introduced the caravel. The early versions were small, of around twenty-five tons, and were used for fishing in the Atlantic. As well as the carvel hulls, where the timbers met flush rather than overlapping each other, the later caravels had multiple masts. The most common arrangement was for a small foremast with a square foresail, a mainmast with a sizeable square mainsail and a mizzen that carried a lateen sail. This mizzen sail, developed from the Latin or Mediterranean ships, made the caravel much more manoeuvrable, while the spread of canvas and a sharper hull made her fast. With such vessels, the Portuguese opened up the world, sailing east and further east in their quest for trade and spices.

Although Scotland was not at the forefront of nautical technology, she was not hindmost either and by the late 1440s caravels were common along the East Coast. Andrew Powty of Leith was the first recorded Scottish owner of a caravel, which Alexander Wallace skippered to such good effect that in 1448 he captured a Winchelsea fishing vessel off the Norfolk Coast. The eighteen unfortunate captives were carried to Aberdeen. Although Wallace demanded a ransom of ninety marks, diplomacy between the Scottish and English kings secured the release of the fishermen.

Piracy was always two-sided, with English and

other mariners equally likely to seize a vulnerable Scottish prize. In 1453 *Marie* of St Andrews was one of the largest Scottish vessels. Capable of carrying 125 wine tuns, she carried a crew of thirty, with four merchants, four servants and the shipmaster when English pirates pounced. There are no details of any resistance and three years later, renamed *Antony*, the pirated vessel was carrying virtuous English pilgrims to Spain. Bishop Kennedy of St Andrews, part owner of Marie, may have approved but still attempted, and failed, to retrieve his ship.

The 1470s seem to have been a bad era for Scottish shipping, with English piracy on the increase and little Scottish response. However, King James III ordered that two galleys should be built, and when an English pirate fleet raided the Forth in 1481, Scottish retaliation drove them away. A new generation of Scottish seamen produced names such as Andrew Wood, whose exploits against English pirates were legendary, and the Barton clan who earned a somewhat darker reputation.

Master and probably owner of *Flower*, Wood was a merchant seaman as well as a captain of the king. He had risen from the lowest rank, clambering tenaciously up the ladder of advancement until he was a respected member of the community of Leith. When Lord Howard and Sir Thomas Fulford led another English fleet to the Forth in 1482, Andrew Wood was among the

PIRATES AND PICKLED HEADS

Scottish seamen who sailed out to offer battle. He must have played an important part, for the following year King James granted him lands at Lower Largo, right at the entrance to the Firth. Chartering the royal ship *Yellow Carvel*, Wood continued his career as a merchant, while aiding the king against rebels in 1488.

The rebellion was successful, a new young king was on the throne and Wood sailed on. He defended the Forth against a raiding English flotilla in 1489, carrying the captured pirates into Leith, but next year he faced a sterner challenge. According to Pitscottie the historian, King Henry VII of England believed the defeat of the English fleet was a national affront and selected a fighting captain in Stephen Bull, and three hand-picked crews to take revenge on Wood.

Wood was returning from a trading trip to the Low Countries when Bull emerged from ambush in the lee of the Isle of May. Bull passed round the wine before clearing for action, and the rival ships, three English to two Scots closed. It was hand-to-hand combat as the ships drifted close to shore, where crowds watched the action like spectators at a gruesome sporting occasion. The ships broke apart at night and renewed the battle next morning, only to run aground on the Tay sandbanks. It was Wood who emerged victorious, carrying the English vessels into Dundee. King James IV sent home the officers, while Wood used the common mariners to help with building work around his new castle at Largo.

Despite the actions of Andrew Wood, piracy still flourished in the North Sea, occasionally spilling into the Firth of Forth. It was James IV who ordered Inchgarvie to be fortified to help repel further English or pirate raids, and James IV who commanded that Andrew Barton should sail out to hunt out a collection of Dutch pirates who had captured some Scottish merchant ships and murdered the crews.

As the master of *Margaret*, newly built at the Shore in Leith, Andrew Barton scoured the North Sea for the Dutch. *Margaret* was perhaps the finest ship in Scotland at the time, four-masted, named after the king's first wife and impressively large, but she also drew so much water that she ran aground when she was launched. However, Barton was a seaman from a family of seamen, and he was successful in his quest.

In a period where pity was a scarce commodity, Barton hauled in the Dutch pirates and quickly executed them. As proof of his expertise, he pickled the pirate heads and sent them, neatly packed in a barrel, as a present to the king. Presumably, King James approved, for he picked the same captain to lead a Scottish expedition to the Baltic, where Barton overstepped his orders to help in a

Scandinavian naval war and descended into piracy himself.

The Bartons were a dangerous breed to cross. There was John the father, John the son, Andrew, who appears to have been the most reckless and Robert, who became an astute financier. Father John had commanded a royal carvel for King James III in between intervals of peaceful trading. In 1476 a small fleet of Portuguese had attacked and plundered his ship, setting him adrift in a small boat, so John Barton applied for Letters of Marque from the king to enable him to recoup the alleged £6000 loss. A Letter of Marque was a commission, issued by the Admiral or other authority, licensing the master of a private vessel to attack enemy merchant ships, either as part of a royal war or in reprisal for losses suffered. Although officially termed as privateers, the masters of vessels so armed frequently descended into blatant piracy. It was often difficult to decide where the line was drawn.

Letters of Marque permitted the Bartons to attack Portuguese shipping with perfect legality. Homeward bound from trading in Asia or Africa, the Portuguese would be relaxing when the Scottish seamen pounced. Perhaps it was one of Barton's vessels that brought the African lady who graced the court of King James and presided as Queen over the Royal Tournament.

With the Portuguese one of the world's leading maritime nations, retaliation was inevitable. A Portuguese vessel captured *Lion*, Robert Barton's ship when she was in the harbour at Campveere. When the Portuguese entombed Robert in a dungeon, the Barton's simply renewed their assault on Portuguese shipping.

With this history of independent aggression, it was hardly surprising that the Barton's ran riot in the Baltic. Sent to help the king's kinsman, Hans, they spent two consecutive seasons attacking whom they pleased. However, when King Hans complained to James, the Bartons left these northern waters and returned to their old pursuit of Portuguese baiting. Perhaps there were not enough Portuguese ships in the world, or perhaps Andrew Barton heeded the king's stern warning that there was to be no more aggression against vessels of that nation. It is equally possible that Barton merely became greedy, for he began to target English shipping. By 1512 the English were complaining loudly of Scottish piracy. That year they accused Robert Barton of pirating six English vessels over the last two years, three from the Norfolk coast and the others in the narrow waters of the Channel. Another Scottish pirate, David Falconer of Leith was also alleged to have taken English ships.

However, if the Portuguese were Kings of the Ocean, then the English were the young masters.

Their time of dominance was coming, and they resented Scottish pirates who preyed along their coasts. Lord Thomas Howard and Sir Edward Howard, the future Lord High Admiral of England, set off in two vessels to challenge Barton. They came up with him off the English south coast. Barton was in the 120-ton *Lion*, with forty crew, and was accompanied by the smaller *Jennet* of Pirwyn, which he appears to have liberated from the ownership of King Hans. The fight was long and hard, but Barton was wounded early on. Lying on deck, he encouraged his crew by blowing on a whistle, but when a roundshot killed him, the English closed and boarded. Outnumbered and dispirited with the loss of their captain, the Scots lost. The English towed *Lion* into the Thames as a prize.

Despite the loss of Andrew, the Barton name continued to resound in the piratical records of Scotland. Perhaps it was the next generation of the same family that rose to infamy in the 1520s and 30s when they appeared to be in partnership with the notorious Edinburgh pirate Robert Fogo.

It was around the beginning of 1524 that Fogo's name became known. He was master and part owner of *Martin*, along with Alexander and Robert Barton, when he pirated a Dutch vessel belonging to Albert Wangork. When a more honest group of Edinburgh merchants and mariners complained of

Fogo's depravations, the Lords of Council voiced their disapproval. His career was just beginning, however, for only the next year, along with a Leith mariner named Patrick Barcar, he was again accused of piracy, and late that year both men were ordered to Denmark, accused of pirating a Danish vessel.

The Scots built quite a fearsome reputation for piracy, if occasionally made legal by the possession of a letter of marque, with the English Channel a favoured hunting ground. In 1532 an English merchant named John Chapman was sailing to Bordeaux when the sails of Scottish privateers slipped over the horizon. He subsequently wrote a vivid letter that tells of the reaction. English ships at once fled for sanctuary, with the Scots hotly pursuing Chapman into Fowey. He wrote of another Englishman who related a tale of four Scots ships that captured fourteen English vessels as well as a large Spanish ship that held an English cargo. These Scots were more likely to have been privateers than pirates, as they seemed only to target English ships, allowing another vessel to sail unmolested because she was of distinctive Breton build.

Three of the Scots ships were of 100 tons, the fourth of 160 and they chased another nine English ships into Brest. It seems that French seamen sailed out to the four Scottish vessels with an offer to ransom the English captives 'after the old custom of the sea.' The asking price was twenty shillings for a mariner, twice as much for a master or mate. The Scots still hovered offshore while the negotiations took place, and there may have been more Scots off the Scilly Islands and Land's End, a double prong of Scottish privateers waiting to scour English shipping in the English home seas.

With an English war in 1533, Scottish privateers swarmed south, blockading Tynemouth, and forcing Lindisfarne to again fortify itself against attack. George Wallace and William Clapperton, John Kerr and John Barton, son of Robert, commanded the ships off Tynemouth. By now Wallace was the most notable Scots seaman and King James V's favourite skipper. The Scottish privateers captured a dozen English supply ships, although a further six slipped through to Berwick. The English prepared ships in the Thames, but according to the ambassador of the Holy Roman Empire, refused to leave port for fear of capture by the Scots who snapped up a further fifteen English prizes.

It will probably never be known if Fogo was involved in those escapades, but his career continued. In 1530 he was the victim of Dutch or Friesland aggression and by 1539 had obtained Letters of Marque to retaliate. The documents granted him the right to detain any vessel of these nations that came into a Scottish port until he gained compensation, but Fogo, like Andrew Barton before him, overstepped the mark. Cruising off Fair Isle, he captured three Dutch fishing vessels, carried them to England and sold them for an excellent profit. He must have been quite pleased when he returned to Scotland, but less happy when the authorities arrested him for piracy and clapped him in jail.

That was the last heard about Fogo, but his legacy continued. Daunted in the east, the English further provoked Scotland by sending a warship up the west coast to 'punish wild Scots' possibly in an attempt to prevent Hebridean galleys from pirating those parts of Ireland that England claimed. The English ship *Mary Willoughby* sailed into the tangled islands, secure in her size and ranked cannon, but Hector MacLean of Duart had his own nautical pride and his galley fleet captured the English vessel. In time *Mary Willoughby* became part of the Scottish navy, commanded by George Wallace. The following year Highland galleys swarmed around *Mary Walsingham* of Yarmouth as she fished off Shetland, and she too became a prize.

So, it can be seen that Scottish seamen were both predators and victims at that period. While other nations, notably England, sent vessels to plunder Scottish ships, Scottish pirates and privateers were more than capable of holding their own against foreign ships and even raided enemy ports. There was undoubtedly no Caledonian cringe and no thought of allowing any enemy to dictate to Scotland, on sea or on land.

In the meantime an English king sought a Scottish bride for his son, and a Hebridean chief allowed the rest of the world to eat.

NAUTICAL WOOING AND KISMUIL'S GALLEY

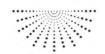

To most people, finding a suitable daughter-in-law should be a pleasurable experience, and perhaps it was for Henry VIII of England, although his methods of wooing a bride would be viewed as unconventional by anybody other than an English king. Although James V of Scotland was Henry's nephew, the English king decided that it would be best to persuade James to marry his daughter to an English prince by burning everything Scottish that he could. Accordingly, English armies crossed the Border to kill, plunder and destroy, while English fleets ravaged Scottish merchant shipping.

In 1542 Vice Admiral John Cary led an English fleet to blockade the Scottish coast while another English fleet sailed from the south. Although much weaker than the English, Scots ships retaliated, with

PIRATES AND PICKLED HEADS

Mary Willoughby and Salamander capturing nineteen English vessels off Northumberland and a small Scottish squadron snatching Henry VIII's wine fleet as it sailed to England from Bordeaux.

In 1544 an English fleet scoured the Forth and burned Leith, so the Scottish ships sought revenge up and down the English coast. Mary Willoughby, Lion and Andrew, owned by the Dundee mariner Andrew Sands, took an unknown number of English prizes, and perhaps were involved in the attack on the English and Dutch fishing fleets off Yarmouth. Despite the fierce war with the English, Scottish mariners could not resist the temptation to turn pirate when the occasion offered, and as well as the Dutch, the Swedes also suffered from Scottish piracy.

Having lost numbers of vessels, the King of Sweden issued Letters of Marque to his own seamen, allowing them to take revenge on Scottish shipping, but after battling with the English, the Scots were not afraid of Scandinavian seamen. It seems that the Swedes were unsuccessful in curbing Scottish piracy, for only four years later they reported that 'terrible great damage is done to Swedish trade by the Scots and English.' National enemies or not, there was little to choose between Scot and Englishman at sea.

In the meantime, the Scots continued with their maritime war with England. Scottish ships cruised the northeast coast of England, menacing Scarborough in October, capturing the 80-ton *Anthony* of Newcastle in November and taking another half dozen coasters later that month. Unable to boast mastery of their own seas, the English gritted their teeth, losing ships and confidence as the Scots roamed seemingly at will, even recapturing a cargo of wool that the English had looted from Leith.

When the Emperor Charles of Austria befriended the English against the Scots and French, Scottish ships sailed to Brittany, lifting the Emperor's vessels with even more ease than they had harried the English. With Scots and French ships clearing the Channel of English shipping, Henry VIII called up a major effort. He demanded action, gathered together a vast fleet that the Scots, for all their daring, could not match for firepower and numbers, and despatched it to the Forth.

In 1547 the English launched a massive land invasion, sweeping aside the Scottish defence at Pinkie, ravaging Edinburgh and Leith, burning, pillaging, and destroying everything that they could not steal or kill. The English retook *Mary Willoughby* and captured Dundee, dominating both Forth and Tay. When English vessels seized three Scots ships, *Lion, Lioness* and the intriguingly named *Marie Celeste* off Norfolk, England appeared to be in the ascendancy.

PIRATES AND PICKLED HEADS

However, it was now that the Auld Alliance held firm as French vessels and French troops reinforced the Scottish war effort. Despite all the efforts of Henry and all the savagery of the English army, Scotland pulled through, gradually pushing the English garrisons out of the country. Perhaps it was not surprising that there were Bartons among the next generation of Scottish seamen to challenge English maritime domination.

In 1548 the Bartons had been involved with a Leith skipper named John Davidson who had captured English shipping. Davidson seems to have been the leader, for he was ordered to bring 'an English prisoner taken in woman's clothes' as well as the ship he captured her in, on pain of a hefty fine. Presumably, Davidson was mingling private enterprise with national war. The following year Davidson and the Bartons were again acting against the English, this time in Aberlady Bay, but once more a Scottish skipper crossed the fine line between privateering and pure piracy, and in 1551 Davidson was hanged at Leith. Even though the French were Scotland's allies, Davidson had pirated a French ship at Bordeaux.

Many other pirates were operating off the Scottish East Coast. One was Robert Isteid of Hastings, who captured a brace of Dutch vessels, let the crews free and took his prizes into Montrose. However, two of the Dutch seamen, Herman and Cornelius

Jonnesoun, had mounted horses and followed Isteid's ship. They immediately informed the authorities what had happened. Another account of the same story claims that the prizes were Scots and Isteid was driven into Montrose by a storm, but the outcome was the same; Isteid was hanged at Leith along with his crew. More intriguingly one was Peter Fisher, a Leith mariner who had sailed with Hawkins.

Sometimes pirates became involved with affairs of state. In 1567, after a period of tangled romance and politics, the Earl of Bothwell, one-time lover, and husband of Queen Mary, fled the mainland for Orkney. Unscrupulous by nature, Bothwell teamed up with the notorious pirates Adam Blacader and David Witter, but the Lords who ruled Scotland in the absence of a monarch sent a flotilla in pursuit of the runaway Earl. Commanded by William Kirkcaldy of Grange, William Murray of Tullibardine and Andrew Lamb of Leith, the four government ships caught up with Bothwell off Orkney.

The pirates fled, the government ships pursued, but *Unicorn*, the leading ship, struck a rock and by the time Kirkcaldy of Grange saved his men, Blacader and Witter had transported Bothwell to Shetland and the hospitality of Olaf Sinclair. As Bothwell fled to Denmark, an extended imprisonment and eventual death, the government ships pursued the pirates. They caught Witter and another pirate with the familiar name of Fogo; blood told in old nautical Scotland.

As the sixteenth century dragged to a close, the North Sea was no safer for shipping. In the seven years between 1572 and 1579, English pirates attacked over twenty Scottish vessels, while townsfolk in Berwick in Tweed openly consorted with pirates, to the fury of the Scots. Nevertheless, however bad things were in the east, they were positively chaotic in the west.

While many of the pirates along the East Coast were English, it was Scotsmen who ravaged the western seas. Leonard Robertson of Kirkcudbright was a feared name in the Irish Sea, supported by many of the local lairds to whom he sold his booty. It is possible that Lord Maxwell, the West March Warden, was even encouraging his piracy. However, the more responsible and sober men of the Town Council, who may have depended on trade for their income, hoped to free Kirkcudbright of the 'men of weir and marinaris' who spoiled the peace with their 'tulzeing and harlotrie.' When the English Queen Elizabeth, who was not averse to setting her own pirates loose on innocent Spanish seamen, complained, King James VI ordered an enquiry. Perhaps it was not surprising that Robertson should be acquitted when his judges were alleged to be the same lairds who bought the spoils of his pirating.

Nevertheless, Robertson was only one fish in a small pond, and other Scottish pirates achieved much more lasting notoriety. One of the most famous, and a man about whose exploits songs are still sung, was Ruari Og MacNeil of Barra. He was the hero of the song Kismuil's Galley, the island chief whose vessels raided the coast of Ireland and snatched English vessels that dared the western seas.

There are many colourful tales about Ruari MacNeil, relating to his nautical skill and pride. One such refers to the Barra tradition of MacNeil eating and then sending a herald to the top of Kismuil Castle, where he proclaimed to the world:

'Hear o ye people! And listen, o ye nations! The Great MacNeil of Barra, having finished his meal, the princes of the earth may dine!'

Barra is the most southern large island in the 120-mile long chain, which make up the Outer Hebrides. At twenty square miles, it is not huge, but it has a unique beauty and a deserved reputation for hospitality. At the end of the sixteenth and the beginning of the seventeenth century, the only reputation it had was for piracy. It was a time of anarchy amounting nearly to chaos in the Hebrides. The old order was gone, wiped away by the Scottish Crown's removal of the Clan Donald

PIRATES AND PICKLED HEADS

Lordship of the Isles, and rival clans battled for supremacy or survival. Sitting snug in the Lowlands, Stuart Kings manipulated events by setting their pet clans against the rest. While the more independent-minded clans resisted, those who were more pliant knuckled down or thrived under their Lowland king. Chief of these were the Campbells, Gordons, and Mackenzies, but the MacNeils of Barra had their own boat and steered their own course.

At one time the MacNeils had followed Clan Donald as had nearly every Hebridean clan, and at the ugly sea battle of Bloody Bay in 1480 they chose the losing faction in what was basically a MacDonald civil war. Now they owed allegiance to nobody.

Chief of the Barra MacNeils was Roderic, known in Gaelic as Ruairi 'n Tartair: Ruairi the Turbulent, and if he thought of himself as a dignified chief equal to the princes of the earth, the feeling was not reciprocated. His reputation was that of a pirate; daring, possibly colourful, but savage.

'As for the Highlands' wrote King James VI 'I shortly comprehend them all in two sorts of people; the one, that dwelleth in our mainland that are barbarous, and yet mixed with some show of civility; the other that dwelleth in the Isles and are all utterly barbarous.'

These were interesting words from a king about his own people.

The utterly barbarous Ruairi was proud of his taste in wine. At all times, he claimed, the wine cellars of his castle of Kismuil were full. Some of this wine, possibly most, was pirated from ships foolish enough to come within range of his galleys. That meant anywhere south of Cape Wrath and west of the Scottish mainland, plus the coasts of Ireland and the Irish Sea. The Irish knew MacNeil well. 'Reputedly the best seafaring warrior in the islands' wrote the Dean of Limerick 'I have heard some of MacNeil's sept to have come with the Malleys to prey on Valentia; an island in M'Cartymore's Country.' Like the other Hebridean mariners, MacNeil used a galley or a fleet of galleys. Also called a lymphad, from long fada, Gaelic for longship, this was an open vessel derived in part from the Viking longboat and possibly from the nyvaig or little ship, of Somerled. Clinker built with a single central mast carrying a square lugsail, the galley had a rudder aft of the sternpost, two dozen, or more, oars of pine and a large crew. As they rowed, the oarsmen sang an iorram, a rowing song, to keep the stroke and make the tedious task more comfortable.

Although the Hebrideans used archers well into the seventeenth century, the galley's favourite tactic was to close, grapple and board, relying on speed, ferocity, and weight of numbers. They were fast, not always easy to handle and required some skill to master in the rough western seas. Ruairi had an abundance of that skill.

It was when he targeted English shipping that royalty began to take note. Possibly it was MacNeil himself who commanded the galley that captured the Dutch and French ships, or even the English merchantman in the Irish Sea. It may have been a MacNeil galley that in 1580 pirated *White Hart* of Bridgewater in Somerset, with its cargo worth some thousands of pounds. Unfortunately, Elizabeth's virgin Queen heard and again demanded action from King James.

Although King James did not act sternly against Robertson, he had his own reasons for wishing to daunt the Hebrideans, He also had no desire to anger Elizabeth; after all, he wanted her throne. So he summoned the MacNeil to his court in Edinburgh. He might as well have summoned the tide for all the notice Ruairi took. After a period of waiting, James realised that his royal command was not enough and whistled up one of his Gaelic allies to help.

Ruairi Mackenzie of Coigach, Tutor of Kintail, was an excellent choice. Devious, uncompromising, reputedly cruel; he had all the attributes necessary to thrive in James' Scotland, plus a knowledge of the Hebrides. A saying of the time claimed that there were only two things worse than the Tutor of Kintail: frost in spring and mist in the dog days of summer. Mackenzie heard James' problem and began to scheme.

After the Hebrideans pirated their targets, they ransacked them for the wine, which provided the mainstay of long alcoholic binges. It was not until 1622 that the Privy Council ordered that in future, vessels passing by the Isles should not carry wine. Mackenzie loaded his barque with bottles of the stuff, ankers of the best French wine he could find —and Scotland had a thriving trade with France. Then he picked a crew of fighting men who would do as they were told and sailed for Barra.

Few ships willingly entered Castlebay, so the Cockman, the officer who acted as sentry-cum-doorman for MacNeil, must have been surprised to see Mackenzie's vessel cruise calmly in and drop anchor outside Kismuil Castle. The ship sat there, swinging gently, her reflection undulating with the quiet waters of the bay. There was little sign of life on deck. The Tutor must have been a man of steady nerve to enter the harbour of a known pirate. And Kismuil, square on its little island in Castlebay, was an '…excellent strength…' According to an account of the 1570s, with '…na passage to the place but be the sea, quairof the entrie is narrow…' (no passage to the place except by the sea, whereof the entry is narrow.'

There might have been lymphads drawn up around Kismuil, a row of sleek craft with their sails furled and oars inboard. Perhaps men were working on them and stopped to stare at this fool who came in. High-pitched laughter hung on the air. The Cockman would issue a challenge as Mackenzie stood on the deck. Now was the time for the Tutor's guile. Speaking swiftly, he praised the MacNeil chief, acclaiming his fame, appealing to his pride.

The Cockman listened, joined in time by MacNeil himself.

'We've come from Norway' the Tutor explained 'bound for Ireland.' That was plausible; Scotland and Norway had a firm trading partnership.

'But why stop here?' MacNeil wondered, assessing the value of the ship for plunder.

'Because we heard of the fame of MacNeil of Barra and we would like to meet him. Oh, by the way, we met a Frenchman the other day. Friendly fellow. We spoke for a while, and we bought some of his wine. Excellent vintage. Perhaps the MacNeil would like to step aboard and sample some?'

The MacNeil would.

Accompanied only by his bodyguard, Ruairi left Kismuil to board the barque. The Tutor proved a good host, plying his guests with the wines from his hold. Wine, and more wine, until MacNeil and his bodyguard, were too stupefied to resist.

Then the Tutor pounced. An arranged sign brought in his ruffians who had been hiding under loose hatches; the MacNeil chief and his man were dragged away, the bodyguard put ashore and MacNeil tossed below. The hatches were secured, and the barque hoisted sail.

Miraculously there was no pursuit, and in time Ruairi found himself in Edinburgh, face to face with the king. Where MacNeil saw an intelligent, ornately dressed but nervous man, James saw a seaman, tall, good looking, elderly and benign with a long grey beard, whose every tall inch proclaimed him a chief.

As MacNeil had no Scots and the king did not speak Gaelic, the ever-helpful Tutor volunteered to act as translator.

James asked why MacNeil persisted in 'pyracies and robbrys' against Queen Elizabeth's subjects.

MacNeil looked astonished and explained that he was only showing his anger at the execution of James mother, Queen Mary, by Elizabeth's orders.

Fair enough. The king did not seem displeased with the reply. Rather than hang MacNeil, he said 'the devil take the carle! Rory, take him with you again and dispose of him and his fortune as you please.' After that, James took away MacNeil's lands and presented them to the Tutor. Who promptly handed them back to MacNeil, but with Mackenzie as the feudal superior, entitled to an annual rent of forty pounds Scots, a hawk, and the use of MacNeil's armed power.

So although MacNeil lost a little of his freedom, he continued to launch his galleys into the western sea. However, he was only one of many pirates in those waters.

PIRATES OF THE HEBRIDES

As the sixteenth century folded into the seventeenth, King James VI attempted to impose Lowland rule on various parts of the Highlands and Islands. As part of this procedure, he handed Lewis over to a consortium that has come down in history as the Fife Adventurers, who were to settle the island, exploit the supposedly fertile soil and fish the seas. Any future land grants north and west of the Highland Line were to be only for Lowlanders or those Highlanders that met with Lowland approval. However, in Lewis, the local MacLeods had not been consulted about this change of ownership, and their reaction was consistently violent. The Lowlanders settled where Stornoway now sits, and the Hebrideans harried their houses on land and their vessels at sea.

PIRATES AND PICKLED HEADS

King James had realised that the Hebrideans might object to this invasion, and he gave the island chiefs fifteen days in which to 'demolische and destroy' their boats. Those Highlanders who resided on the West Coast of the mainland were to hand over their vessels to the Adventurers so they could be used in the Lewis project. The Hebrideans' 12- to 18-oar birlinns and lymphads were fast and dangerously formidable against merchant vessels but were less useful against warships, whose artillery could destroy them at long range. To ensure that the Adventurers were unmolested, neither Hebrideans nor West Coast Highlanders were permitted to build further vessels for three years.

After the initial skirmishes, the main Hebridean resistance fighter was Neil MacLeod, who had fortified the Island of Birsay, to the west of Lewis, and used it as a base for conducting guerrilla warfare that kept the Lowlanders very much on edge. Realising that the Lowlanders were outmatched, King James allowed the Adventurers' claim to Lewis to lapse, and instead handed the island to Mackenzie of Kintail. Mackenzie was more amenable to Lowland law than were the MacLeods, but as a Gael, he was less offensive to the people of the island, and Neil MacLeod began to feel isolated. Rather than a freedom fighter, he had become an outlaw, supported only by the loyal band of followers who were as much outside the king's peace as was he.

It must have been a trying time, waiting on that windswept island, always wondering what the future would bring, so when a ship approached, the MacLeods would have reached for handy weapons, wondering if King James had despatched a warship against them. The ship did not come to Birsay, but sailed to Kirkibost, Bernera, and anchored. These seemed to be no hostile intent, so Neil MacLeod crossed over to see precisely what ship chose to come to these disputed waters. There would be another tense few moments as the Hebrideans closed, pistols ready, swords loose in their scabbards, and the lookout of the alien ship called for the officer of the watch. However, things improved when the captain of the ship introduced himself.

The ship was *Priam*, her captain was an English pirate named Peter Love, and he told Neil about his last voyage. He had been cruising off Ireland, seeking for any vessel that might be foolish enough to cross his bows, but he had to put ashore, no doubt for provisions, or possibly for plunder. Little difference, really, for pirates. Unfortunately, the Irish were not welcoming; some of Love's men were captured, and *Priam* only escaped by luck, and the skill of her captain. Seamen were expendable, of course, and the fewer the crew, the less there were to share the loot they carried.

Pirates were not renowned for their taciturn natures, and soon all of Birsay knew of the precious cargo on *Priam*. There was cinnamon, pepper, cochineal, and ginger, all the rich spices of the East. There was sugar from the West Indies, 700 Indian hides that might have been deerskin, a parcel of muskets, twenty-nine pieces of silver plate and a box of jewels that had once been owned by a Dutchman. Love had decided to search for a safe haven for his cargo, and either through ignorance or blind faith had chosen Lewis.

But perhaps Lewis was not so bad a place for an English pirate. After all, it had a seagoing population that was not averse to illegal adventures, a base defended by the arms of Neil MacLeod and his men, and it was convenient for any ships that used the Northern seas. *Priam* went a-pirating again, to the dismay of Thomas Fleming of Anstruther, whose ship fell victim. While Fleming was made a captive, his vessel was used as a guardship. The irony would surely not have escaped the MacLeods, having a Fife vessel helping guard them against a situation that was instigated by adventurers from Fife. It is unlikely that Fleming would have appreciated the irony. Love also captured a Flemish buss, probably one of the many fishing vessels that exploited Hebridean waters without benefit to Scotland. Hauling five of the crew out of the buss, Love used them as slave labour on *Priam*, while he put some of his own crew on the Flemish vessel. Either these seamen were not competent, or they ran into some nasty weather, for the buss was wrecked on the shore of Shetland.

In the meantime relations between Love and Neil MacLeod remained amicable. They seem to have signed a bond of mutual defence and offence, and island tradition agrees that Love was engaged to marry one of the MacLeod women on Birsay, perhaps a daughter of Torquil Blair MacLeod. However Neil was not an easy man to deal with; maybe he had quarrelled with the pirate captain, or possibly he merely wanted to use the Englishman to improve his own position, but he had treachery in mind.

With at least two successful pirate cruises and a forthcoming wedding to celebrate, it is hardly surprising that there were feasts on Birsay. Love invited the MacLeods to *Priam* and regaled them with the best his ship could offer, so Neil could not do less than return the compliment. He brought the captain and a selected few of the crew over to Birsay, but while they feasted in splendid good fellowship, Torquil Blair MacLeod, the prospective father-in-law, led a party of men to seize *Priam*.

It would be a typical Hebridean night, with the Atlantic breakers thundering on the coast, the sound of merriment from Neil's feast and a sky of ten thousand stars. *Priam* had been safe at anchor for some time now, and the watchman would be off-guard when the Hebrideans came. All the same, the pirates tried to fight, but rather than defenceless merchant seamen they were facing Neil MacLeod's men, some of the most skilled guerrilla fighters in Europe. There was no doubt about the outcome; some of the pirates were killed, the others were captured. The enslaved Dutchmen were released and helped on their way to Lewis, but Neil held onto a stray Scotsman.

Naturally the MacLeods ransacked *Priam*, although her cargo seems to have been left untouched. Perhaps there was little need for cochineal or ginger on Birsay, but silver was always welcome, and tradition claims that the MacLeods raked in a large amount, dividing it between them by the helmet-load. It has been suggested that the knowledge of this treasure inspired Neil's attack on the pirates, which may be a slander on the MacLeod. Or perhaps not.

With *Priam* safely under MacLeod control, Neil informed the Privy Council of his actions. Probably he hoped that he would obtain a pardon, for living the life of an outlaw on an island that was exposed to all the rigours of the Hebridean weather must have been hard. Whatever the Privy Council, safe in Edinburgh, thought of Neil, they sent an agent named Patrick Grieve to take *Priam* and all her fixtures and fittings, to Edinburgh. Nothing was said about the captured coinage, which appears to have been conveniently forgotten.

Captain Love and what remained of his crew were also transported to Edinburgh, although two died on the voyage from wounds received during the fight for the ship. The rest were tried in December 1610. Love came from Lewes in Sussex, and he had four other Englishmen, two Welshmen and an Irishman as piratical companions. To the Privy Council they were all 'wicket Impes of the Devill.' The court had no doubt about their guilt, and they joined the scores of pirates who were hanged at the Sands of Leith.

Despite his hopes for a pardon, Neil was afforded only a temporary reprieve, which he spoiled by returning to his old ways. Once again, he led his followers across the narrow channel between Birsay and Lewis, once again MacLeod broadswords swung against Mackenzie necks. There was fire and blood on the island, and the wails of orphaned children rising to the ragged Hebridean sky. It was Neil himself who shot two Mackenzies who were rash enough to show themselves on the rocks opposite Birsay.

Unable to take Birsay by direct assault without suffering grievous loss to his men, the Tutor of

PIRATES AND PICKLED HEADS

Kintail, Ruari Mackenzie, resorted to the cunning that had served him so well in the past. There were still plenty of MacLeods living on Lewis, and the Tutor rounded up all the women and children who had a blood relation to the outlaws on Birsay. It is a poignant scene, the struggling women, crying children and the rough followers of Mackenzie pushing them across the island to where the Atlantic breaks in fury on the greasy, weed covered rocks. There they were left, well below the high tide mark and within easy sight of their relatives on Birsay.

The followers of Neil would be watching from cover, perhaps identifying individuals from the frightened mass of people. They would know exactly when the tide would turn and how long it would take to cover the rocks on which their people stood. Sending across a man in a small boat, the Tutor ordered Neil to surrender or watch the women and children drown.

At first, the MacLeods might have thought it a bluff, but not for long. The Tutor was known as a ruthless, cunning man. He might just allow these people to die. The tide would turn, the surging sea would creep closer to the rocks, then would surround it, and silver spindrift would shower the huddled innocents. There would be screams and a few curses; mothers would lift their children to give them a few minutes more of precious life, and all the time the Tutor would be watching, his men at his back.

'All right' Neil agreed. 'We'll leave Birsay, as long as we can leave Lewis too.' It was not that they did not trust the Tutor, just that they knew him too well. No doubt the women and children were relieved, but there was little safety for the likes of Neil MacLeod. He was accepted into the care of Ruari MacLeod of Harris, a kinsman by name, who intended to take him to seek justice from a higher authority than the Tutor of Kintail. Surely King James VI, down in London, would listen to the tale of a man fighting for his own lands.

It was a long journey from Harris to London, and perhaps the MacLeods would have been better to sail all the way, but they stopped at Glasgow, where the Privy Council ordered that Neil be brought to Edinburgh. The grey city was seldom kind to the Gael, and Neil stood trial before a collection of unsympathetic Edinburgh faces. It was the 30th March 1613 when the charges were read out. Found guilty of fire-raising, burning, theft, murder, and piracy, there could only be one verdict. Neil Macleod, a man of character, bravery and guile who could have been remembered as a Lewis Wallace, was hanged at the Mercat Cross 'ane thaireftir, his heid to be strukin frome his body, and affixt and set upone ane pricket' (thereafter, his head to be struck from his body and affixed and set upon a stake.)

Yet Neil was not a man to bemoan his fate. He knew that his cause was just, for he had only defended his own, and he expected a reprieve from the king, but it was not to be. In April 1613 he walked slowly, hopefully, to the scaffold and one of the executioners, either a Highlander or possessing a modicum of Gaelic, ordered him 'hurry up you old *bodach*'—old man. Neil turned on the man and replied:

'If I were on a ship's deck, where it was difficult to keep one's footing while steering over the billows, you would not call me a bodach, laddie.' It is said that Neil, in a last gesture of defiance, knocked his tormentor down before he was hanged. His head was removed and remained to grin down at Edinburgh from a spike above the Nether Bow Port.

Even with *Priam* removed, MacNeil tamed, and MacLeod hanged, there was no peace in the west. Other pirates abounded. The Morrisons were historically based at Ness, in the far north of Lewis, and their chief was the hereditary Judge or Brieve of that island. Sometime toward the end of the sixteenth century, Brieve John Morrison of Lewis was steering his galley northward to Rona. The Brieve was in the stern, no doubt at his ease enjoying the bracing weather, while his crew, perhaps fifty strong, were hauling at the long oars to the accompaniment of a rowing song. They were making fine progress when someone sighted a Dutch sail.

Any vessel in these waters was fair game, so the galley pulled up alongside, and the Morrisons boarded. It must have been quite a shock for the Dutchman, one minute to be ambling along peacefully in northern waters, the next to have two score howling Hebrideans bounding along the deck with the steel of dirks and claymores gleaming dull and dangerous.

The pirated ship was steered to Ness, on the northern tip of Lewis, and there would be delight to find that her cargo was wine. At this time there seems to have been an alliance between Clan MacAuley and the MacLeods of Lewis, which worried the Brieve. Rather than squander such a prize on a drunken spree, the Brieve invited some of his enemies to a reconciliation feast, or so it would appear as Torquil MacLeod, Alister MacLeod of the small heel, and Donald Cam MacAuley arrived at Ness. Set against the background of the heaving Atlantic, the Dutch ship would be riding at anchor, with a good portion of her cargo unloaded and distributed around the captain's cabin for everybody to sample. What better way to end a feud than with a celebration? The guests came on board and sat down to test the vintage. As it was a peaceful meeting, everybody's weapons were stored in the vessel's arms chest, which would ensure that any arguments would not end in bloodshed.

At first, all went well. The initial suspicion would dissipate under the influence of alcohol, old enmities would fade as bitter enemies became first wary rivals, then companions of the bottle. However, Donald Cam MacAuley was nobody's fool. Like so many Lewismen, he understood the sea, so when the motion of the ship altered, he realised that something was wrong. Making an excuse to go on deck, he saw that the cable had been quietly cut, sails stealthily raised and now Ness was astern, and the ship was steering eastward, toward the Scottish mainland. 'Torquil!' he shouted, 'We are betrayed!'

But when Torquil reached for the arms room, all the weapons had been removed. Ready to fight barehanded, the visitors found that the Brieve had crammed the holds with Morrisons, who surged on deck and overpowered the visitors. Donald Cam was a warrior, hard to control, but among the Brieve's followers was one John Roy Mackay of Bragar, a huge man of muscles and might. He fell on the unarmed Donald, overpowered him by sheer strength, and tied him to the mast. To ensure that the pinioned man could create no mischief, a group of Morrisons held their swords to his body.

Helpless, Donald watched as Torquil Og MacLeod was also pinioned and tied.

The ship sailed for Loch Broom, where Torquil was taken away, while Donald Cam and Alister MacLeod were chained together by their feet. Once this was done, the same chain was passed around the neck of Donald. All the other prisoners were likewise chained together in pairs before being placed in a secure prison. There was no doubt that the Brieve intended to kill them, probably after the semblance of a trial to make it appear lawful, so there were heavy hearts at the aftermath of the feast.

It was perhaps a night or two later, as the prisoners sat with their backs to the wall, that an old man appeared among them, offering each of the condemned a plant that he had plucked from the seashore. Although most of the prisoners ignored the old man, Donald Cam accepted one of the plants, as did Alister MacLeod. The next day the Brieve arranged a mock trial for the prisoners, and the hangings began. Torquil Og met his end there, strung up by the neck with his face toward Loch Broom and perhaps seeing Lewis beyond. A pair of prisoners were hanged every morning, until one night only two remained. But Alister was not known as 'small heel' for nothing. He knew that his feet were of different sizes and he had been steadily working the smaller free of the links of the chain.

Free, he looped the remains of the chain over the head of Donald Cam, and between them, they broke open the door of the jail and escaped.

However, escaping from jail was easier than escaping from the mainland. The Brieve had powers of law and order over the area and gave orders that every boat was to be turned upside down, and each oar was to be kept indoors so that the fugitives could not escape. The escapees travelled down the coast as hunted men, until in Applecross they found the remains of what had once been a boat, lacking oars and with the seams agape with age. But Donald Cam was resourceful; handfuls of clay were used to caulk the seams, and he broke two planks of wood from a cattle-pen to use as oars.

They were rowing toward Skye when the weight of the chains that still hung around his neck proved too much for Donald Cam. Even his great strength was spent, and he could only sit in the stern sheets while Alister rowed on, single-handed, stopping every so often to bale, for the clay was not proof against the waves of the western ocean. Alister asked why Donald was not rowing, to which he replied that he hoped for an argument by which both would perish.

'And let the Brieve win?'

Alister continued to row until they reached Dunvegan, home of the chief of the Skye MacLeods.

A helpful smith removed the chain, and Donald and Alister borrowed a more seaworthy vessel for the sail to Harris and then to their home in Uig. After that, it was time for vengeance. It is said that John Mor Mackay kept on the alert in Dun Bragar, but Donald evaded the defences and killed him in bed. The Morrisons also suffered, for although many hid in the great broch at Dun Carloway, Donald carried bundles of heather to the top, set them alight and dropped them inside. It was a fiery death for the pirates of Lewis.

There are other versions of this story, in some of which the ship was taken to Stornoway, in others, there was no Dutch ship at all, but the Brieve entertained Donald Cam in his own galley, or delivered Torquil Dhu MacLeod to his brother and enemy Torquil Conanach in Coigach. Nonetheless, the idea is similar, and the story conveys some of the atmosphere of life for some in the sixteenth century Hebrides.

Of course, not every pirate was Hebridean, and not every visit ended in execution and fire. Sometimes the pirates were never identified, and their prey was more prosaic than French wine or Spanish Gold. In one notable occasion, the pirates were hunting for birds' eggs. Perhaps birds' eggs have little value now, but to the people of St Kilda, they were the bread and staff of life. St Kilda is a paradise for birds, with gannets, fulmar, and puffin nesting on the magnificent steep cliffs of the island, and it was on these cliffs that the men of the island hunted them. It was a dangerous, highly skilled job for the St Kildeans, being lowered down the cliffs with the surging Atlantic hundreds of feet below and the whirling, screaming sea birds all around. No wonder the men of the island were among the most highly skilled cragsmen in the world. It is equally of little surprise that they valued the eggs that were won at such considerable risk.

Toward the end of the seventeenth century, the people of the island stared as a strange ship sailed up to their home, and unknown men rowed a small boat to the beach. Very few people ever visited the island, for there was nothing worth plundering; indeed St Kilda was so poor that the inhabitants were exempt from fighting for the clan chief. Yet although they were not a warlike people, their anger was aroused when these intruders began to steal the birds' eggs on which they depended for food.

The whole population of the island fell on the invaders, and there was a wild scrimmage on the shore of Hirta. Few details have survived, but it is known that the islanders won, and some say that the women of the island removed the breeches of the foreign seamen, so they retreated with no eggs and less dignity. The laughter of the St Kilda women must have rivalled the mocking calls of the birds as the pirates sailed away.

Another local pirate was Malcolm MacRuiari MacLeod, who the Mackenzies had chased from Lewis. With the home of his ancestors denied to him, he chose to make a dishonest living on the sea and became involved in the Clan Donald rebellion of 1615, when the MacDonalds of Dunyveg in Islay attempted to regain their lands from Argyll's Campbells. Contemporary accounts speak of 'eighty broken Highland men' with a 'bark and some birlinns' pirating boats between Scotland and Ireland. By June of that year, there were 300 Hebrideans, but when the Earl of Argyll moved in, the uprising collapsed. Malcolm MacLeod teamed up with Coll MacGillespic, and the two wild men roamed the western seaboard, terrorising honest seafarers, and taking a swipe at Clan Campbell whenever the opportunity presented itself.

News of these events reached the Privy Council in Edinburgh, who issued a writ of Fire and Sword against the pirates and a reward of 3000 merks for the capture of Malcolm MacRuiari MacLeod. With every man's hand against them, the band split up, and Malcolm MacLeod escaped to Ireland, where the MacDonalds held lands in the Glens of Antrim. The Edinburgh authorities sent Captain David Murray to clear the Hebrides of pirates.

However, Malcolm MacLeod itched for the sea,

and he soon returned to infest the Hebrides. This time the full power of Clan Campbell was turned against him, while the infamous Tutor of Kintail was watching for him in Lewis. It seemed that the Hebrides were closed to him, so Malcolm sailed away to the Low Countries for another break, before once again returning to his homeland. At this time, the Hebrides were in a ferment, with the Mackenzies having usurped MacLeod power in Lewis while the Campbells grabbed Islay from the Macdonalds, so it was easy for Malcolm MacLeod to find men as desperate as himself. Teaming up with Sorley MacDonald and his homeless Islaymen, Malcolm pirated a French ship that was foolish enough to sail the Western Ocean.

Leaving the Campbell-dominated waters of the southern Hebrides, Malcolm and the MacDonalds began hunting around Lewis, helped by MacLeod of Harris, who must have been nervous of the intentions of his Mackenzie neighbour. It was a Harris MacLeod who informed Malcolm of a ship then anchored at Stornoway. A Lowland ship owned or captained by one Robert Alexander of Burntisland in Fife, she would be a prime target, particularly as men from Fife men had intended taking Lewis from the MacLeods.

Being Hebrideans they used every advantage they could, creeping up to the Fife vessel by night in an 8-oared boat, and boarding her before the

Lowlanders were aware of their presence. There were forty Hebrideans, well-armed with muskets, dirks, and targes, and it was midnight when they fell on the sleeping crew. The Fifers were no cowards, and they fought back, but taken by surprise in a supposedly peaceful anchorage they had no chance. Alexander was among the wounded, but none of the Fifers was killed; they were not perceived as enemies.

For some reason, Malcolm had a personal grudge against John Mackenzie, the piper of Kintail, and led twenty men in a night-time commando raid on his house at Ranish. There was seldom mercy in these Hebridean feuds, and the piper was butchered as he slept, while some of his followers who attempted to interfere were casually killed. The house was destroyed, bright flames from the thatch rising high in the Lewis night, and Malcolm slipped back to the ship. With his forty thieves straining at the oars, the Fife ship was towed back to where Malcolm's own vessel waited, and the pirates spent a cheerful if sweaty, time transferring the cargo from one ship to the other. All in all, it had been a successful night, a vessel captured, an enemy killed in as neat a raid as was possible to conceive and now a cargo of wine and general merchandise to sell in Dunvegan. Malcolm MacLeod had much to be cheerful about as he resumed his career in piracy. Unlike many

Hebridean pirates, he retired un-hanged and tradition states that he settled in Ireland sometime in the 1620s. It was a happy ending for Malcolm, although his victims may not have been so pleased. As the Scottish western seaboard reeled under the pirate plague, other areas of the world were equally affected, with Scots playing their part.

SCOTTISH PIRATES

NORTH SEA TO THE CARIBBEAN

By the seventeenth century, the focus of maritime power had shifted. Although they still boasted a maritime empire, the Portuguese were no longer the leading nautical nation. Spain, France, England, and the Netherlands contested that honour, as battle fleets clashed in European waters and there was never peace in the waters of the New World. Although Scotland was never a significant sea power, Scottish ships and seamen were heavily involved in this war of titans, sometimes on one side, often on both.

The seventeenth century started as the sixteenth had ended, with piracy along the Scottish coasts. In 1609 the Englishman Captain Perkins, together with his mate William Randall, captured a Dutch vessel, renamed her *Iron Prize,* and began to pirate Scottish

PIRATES AND PICKLED HEADS

shipping. When the threat became known, three ships left Leith to hunt down the pirates. *Iron Prize* captured at least two Scottish vessels, then sailed into Kirkwall in Orkney to obtain supplies. It was there that the Leith ships found her and, after only a brief skirmish, made a prize of Prize. The pirate hunters brought her home in triumph, and a large crowd watched as twenty-seven pirates dangled from the gallows 'within the floodmark' at Leith. Probably of more interest to their captors, the cargo was auctioned for over £13,000.

Sometimes foreign wars intruded into Scottish waters. One such event occurred in Leith when the war between Spain and the Netherlands disrupted the peace of Leith. In June 1622, a Spanish vessel from Dunkirk was granted permission to provision at Leith but was attacked there by a small Dutch fleet. When all four vessels ran aground, the Spaniard informed the Scottish Privy Council what was happening, and cannon were dragged from Edinburgh Castle to enforce the peace. For eleven months there was a wary stand-off, with the authorities supporting the Spanish and the people of Leith on the side of the Protestant Dutch. It was May 1623 before the Spanish agreed to leave the port, but the Leith pilot, by accident or design, steered them onto a sandbank. A second attempt had the same result, and when the Spanish murdered the pilot, the people of Leith only watched when the Dutch attacked and captured the Spaniard. The Leith mob looted the Spanish ship before the Dutch set her on fire. Those Spaniards who made it ashore were attacked and stripped by the locals in a display of savagery as ugly as anything in the Hebrides.

By 1626 England was at war with Spain again, and this time the Spaniards could legally target Scottish ships, as Scotland and England shared the same monarch. Never loath to refuse an opportunity for profit, the Scottish authorities licensed several privateers, who did sterling work while the tiny Scottish navy sat idle in the Forth. Among the better-remembered privateers were *Blessing of God*, skippered by John Morton, and *Archangel*, with William Robertson as captain. Dundee vessels such as *James of Dundee*, skippered by William Forrester, and *Golden Lion of Dundee*, with Thomas Auchinleck as captain, were also issued with Letters of Marque.

Piracy and privateering continued as a recurring theme of maritime life that century. In 1649, following the civil wars in the British Isles, the Estates authorised 'Captain Johne Gillespie' of the 'schip callit the *Elizabeth* of Kirkcaldie to protect, secur and defend all the merchand schips of the kingdome' against 'the violence and wrongs of the Irish frigotts and piratts.' (The ship called *Elizabeth* of Kirkcaldy to protect, succour and defend all the merchant ships of the kingdom against the violence and wrongs of the Irish frigates and pirates.)

By the middle of the 1660s, Scottish privateers were locked in a vicious nautical war with the Dutch. In December 1665, the king granted his gracious permission for the Admiral of Scotland to issue warrants for privateers, and again the seaports sent out their ships. In June 1666, John Masterton of *Providence* of Dundee sallied out to hunt the enemy, joined later that year by Walter Rankine, master of *Christian* of Dundee, soon joined by *Wemyss* of Burntisland. There were another twenty-one known Scottish privateers scouring the seas in the summer of that year, sailing from the ports of Fife and the Tay, from Lothian and Leith, the old seagoing heartland of Scotland. Unfortunately, history is silent about the exploits of these mariners. However, *Lamb* of Leith, skippered by John Brown, was one of the most successful. In July 1666 Brown captured a timber carrier and a vessel laden with wine, both of whom were carried triumphantly into Leith. Another Leith seaman boasted the famous name of Wood, and his ship *Anthony* captured nine prizes in the North Sea. Altogether thirty prize vessels were brought to Leith that summer, but the following year was even better.

With Scottish ships hovering off Spain and France, some of the prizes were of five hundred tons or more, too large to enter most of the Scottish ports. Ships from Leith captured thirteen enemy vessels by April, with one privateer bringing home an East Indiaman with a cargo of silk, probably the greatest treasure ever captured by a Scottish mariner of that period.

The Dutch and their French and Danish allies were also busy, with their warships and privateers adept at capturing unarmed Scottish merchantmen. Although the bulk of Scottish trade came from the East Coast ports, the Clyde was beginning to realise that its future lay in the sea-road to the New World. After losses to Dutch vessels, a group of Glasgow merchants, together with Sir George Maxwell of Newark, grouped together and bought *George*, a sixty-ton vessel. Purchasing Letters of Marque from the Duke of Lennox, Lord High Admiral of Scotland, they appointed Robert McAllan as master, recruited sixty seamen and set her loose on the king's enemies for the sake of the nation and their own profit. Operating from Newark, as the Clyde at Glasgow was too shallow for seagoing vessels, *George* captured several Dutch vessels. One ship may not have altered the balance of power, but *George* pointed a finger to a maritime future that would blossom in the following century. Ships from the Clyde would make their mark on the world.

That Dutch War ended with the Peace of Breda, but the next started in 1672, and again the

PIRATES AND PICKLED HEADS

privateers were busy. With the new Lord High Admiral, the Duke of York, issuing Letters of Marque until his wrist ached, Scots ships patrolled off Heligoland and the Kattegat. They earned so fearsome a reputation that the Dutch 'complained of the cruel usage of the Scotch privateers, which plunder all they meet.' It seems that, once again, Scottish privateers found it challenging to distinguish between legal privateering and sheer piracy. As in all previous wars, the Forth ports in general and Leith, in particular, saw the spars of captured vessels puncturing the grey skies.

The Dutch wars eventually ended, but there was always the French to fight. The seventeenth century ended as it had begun, with bloodshed on the high seas and armed ships cruising for plunder. The privateers in the closing years of the century included Ninian Gibson, who sailed the 100-ton *Lamb* of Glasgow to 'take, seize upon, and apprehend and...sink or destroy the ships and goods of the French, Irish or Scottish Highlands in rebellion.' However, another Scottish mariner was also out hunting, and his name has been recorded as one of the most notorious pirates of all.

Ironically, William Kidd may not have been a pirate at all. He certainly started out as a respectable privateer, hailing originally from either Greenock or Dundee, where the name Kidd was well known in maritime circles. He was a successful merchant by 1690 when he arrived in New York, but there was already a shadow against his name.

According to legend, in 1689 Kidd sailed on board the pirate vessel *Blessed William*, which surrendered at Nevis in the Caribbean, on condition that the crew was pardoned. Using the old maxim of setting a thief to catch a thief, the governor then issued a Letter of Marque to the pirates, and they sallied forth to continue their career, but as honest men and with Kidd as captain. *Blessed William* helped capture and plunder *Marie Galante*, then fought yard arm to yard arm with French men-o'-war, but such deeds were too dangerous for pirates, who sought easy plunder. When Kidd was ashore on private business, the crew, led by Robert Culliford, pirated the vessel, and sailed away, once more 'on the account.'

Naturally incensed, Kidd obtained a government vessel named *Antigua* and hunted for the pirates. During the chase he arrived in New York, where he met the wealthy widow, Sarah Cox, his future wife. Seeming to forget about his quest for Culliford, Kidd settled down, purchased a pew at Trinity Church, bought a house on Wall Street and indulged in some minor privateering. It seems that Kidd desired command of a King's frigate, and in 1695 he crossed the Atlantic to London, where instead he was offered a commission to hunt the notorious Red Sea pirates.

PIRATES AND PICKLED HEADS

These men were the scourge of their era, pirates who haunted the Indian Ocean, preying on East India Company vessels and native craft, living in their own communities in Madagascar. Some were cruel, others pretended Christianity, but Kidd agreed to remove the menace, for a share of their plunder. His commission also allowed him to attack the king's enemies, but there was one significant clause that Kidd may have disregarded. 'We do hereby jointly charge and command you, as you will answer the same at your utmost Peril, that you do not, in any manner, offend or molest any of our Friends or Allies, their ships or Subjects.'

Leaving London in the 34-gun *Adventure Galley*, Kidd promptly lost men to the Royal Navy impress service, then crossed to New York to see his wife. In September 1696 he hoisted sails and set out. When fever decimated his men, he recruited more, then seems to have turned pirate when he attacked the pilgrim traffic in the Red Sea. When a British warship defended the pilgrims, Kidd cruised the Indian Ocean, capturing a few minor prizes, skirmishing here and there, and arguing with his crew. He kidnapped a British pilot, fought the Portuguese and his men raped women in the Laccadive Islands. So far Kidd was neither a romantic nor a successful pirate.

It was early in 1698 that Kidd captured the Mughal Emperor's *Queddah Merchant*, which boasted a cargo of true wealth. There were silks, jewels, and muslin, gold in coin and bars, arms and saltpetre, enough to make the voyage profitable, but when he sailed her to Saint Mary's Island off Madagascar, a well-known pirate haunt, he met Robert Culliford. Naturally, the two men were cautious of one another, but amity prevailed over the neck of a bottle, and Kidd seemed not to mind when Culliford departed with most of his crew.

As *Adventure Galley* was leaking badly, Kidd gave her a fiery funeral, renamed *Queddah* as *Adventure Prize*, and eventually sailed her to the Caribbean. At Anguilla, Kidd learned that the government had determined he should be tried for piracy, partly because of pressure from the Mughal Emperor of India, who was already incensed by the capture of one of his daughters by an English pirate. Leaving his ship in a secluded bay in Hispaniola, Kidd loaded part of the cargo onto a sloop and sailed to Boston. After an attempt at bribery failed, Kidd was transported to London, tried for piracy and murder. He was hanged in chains at Wapping.

His death left at least two unanswered questions. Was he a pirate? Indeed he was, for he attacked neutral shipping. The second question is harder to answer and has caused much more speculation over the years: what happened to Kidd's legendary treasure? There have been several abortive hunts for the supposed fabulous wealth that Kidd was supposed to have buried. From Mahone Bay in Nova Scotia to Boston and the Hudson River Valley to the South China Seas, hopeful men have removed vast amounts of topsoil in the pursuit of wealth. None have been successful. It is more than likely that there was no treasure to find, but just possible that, somewhere between Madagascar and Boston, Kidd deposited the remains of the cargo of *Queddah Merchant*. While in Boston he did boast of a treasure worth £50,000, but not much credence should be attached to such words. Although the silks would have long perished, perhaps there are gold bars there, just waiting to be discovered.

Kidd, of course, was not the only Scottish pirate to sail Caribbean waters. Many of the English, Dutch, French, and Spanish vessels carried Scotsmen among their crews, such as Alexander Selkirk, the original of Robinson Crusoe, and there was even the occasional Scottish pirate captain. One such was James Browne, who in 1677 sailed with a French Letter of Marque from Saint Domingue. However the temptation to pirate a stray Dutch slave ship proved strong, and after the pirates killed the captain and crew, they released the slaves in Jamaica. Unfortunately for Browne, his career ended shortly afterwards when a British frigate captured his ship, and he was hanged. Most pirates who did not end their lives in obscurity graced the end of a noose. Of thirty-one pirates who were hanged at one time in Charlestown, South Carolina, three came from Aberdeen and two from Glasgow. Scotsmen were as likely to be pirates in the Caribbean and along the American coast as were seamen from any other nation.

Sometime Scottish pirates even operated off Africa.

BARBARY CORSAIRS AND CLYDESIDE PRIVATEERS

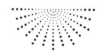

From the Middle Ages until the early nineteenth century, any mariner in the Mediterranean always watched the horizon. From the Levant to the Gut, and especially along the Barbary Coast, piracy was rife and sometimes Scottish ships were captured. Such an event occurred in 1615 when four Leith mariners were sold in the slave market at Algiers. The Scottish Privy Council requested that every church in the country should raise a collection to buy their freedom, a plea that was to become relatively common throughout the century and well into the next. In 1677 the Scottish kirks collected for the crew of *Isabel* of Montrose, who had been sailing home from La Rochelle with a cargo of brandy and salt when a Barbary ship captured them. Hopefully, they were released, but some Scots were destined to remain in Africa for an extended period.

Peter Lisle was a blond Glaswegian who was one of the most noted navigators among the Barbary corsairs. According to legend, Lisle was a seaman on board a Mameluke ship when he was converted to Islam, but it is more likely that he was captured at sea by a Tripoli privateer. Renaming himself Murat Reis, in the autumn of 1796, he was hunting for prey and pirated two American vessels. Later that year the Pasha of Tripoli appointed Lisle as captain of an American prize named *Betsy*. Schooner rigged, she was fast, and Lisle renamed her *Meshuda*, armed her with 28 guns, and fought a Danish frigate to a standstill.

Obviously a good seaman, Lisle rose to admiral and married the pasha's daughter. He seems to have had a personal vendetta with Americans, and in 1800, the year after an American consul settled at Tripoli, he pirated a trio of American ships. Until the American War of Independence, British subsidies and the Royal Navy had protected American vessels, but after 1783 they were fair game for every corsair on the coast. However, not only Americans suffered. When an Algerian Xebec captured the Philadelphian brig *Dolphin* in 1790, four of the American's crew were Scottish. There was Charles Colvile of Arbroath, John Robertson of Glasgow, George Smith of Portsoy, and William

PIRATES AND PICKLED HEADS

Paterson from Aberdeen. Through negotiations with the British consul in Algiers, at least one of the Scots were released, with £350 securing the freedom of Colvile.

By 1801 Tripoli and the United States were at war and Lisle, with two ships, cruised for prey. Unfortunately for him, this time the Americans were in earnest and in June of that year the US vessel *Philadelphia* trapped Lisle's ships at Gibraltar.

However, Lisle was both intelligent and pragmatic. Abandoning his ships, he ushered the crews into small boats and told them to sail to Morocco. Only when they were safe did Lisle hitch a lift on a British ship, disembark at Malta, and cross to Tripoli, where he slipped through the American blockade to organise the city's defences.

As the war continued, Admiral Lisle commanded Tripoli's fleet. He fought USS *Constellation* gun to gun, led a roaring party of boarders to capture Philadelphia in 1803 and endured the United States bombardments of 1804. Given the American views on the British system of impressment, it is interesting to realise that the crew of *Philadelphia* was mainly from Britain. With the end of the war in 1805, Barbary piracy was in decline, but Lisle continued as an interpreter.

Despite the exploits of Lisle, he was not the most famous Scottish pirate of the eighteenth century. That accolade fell to John Smith, better remembered as John Gow. Smith was an Orcadian, so seafaring was as natural to him as breathing. He rose to become second mate and gunner of *George Galley* that sailed around the Mediterranean, but in November 1724 he was the ringleader of a mutiny that seized the ship. It is possible that the men were complaining about ill-treatment on board, and particularly about a shortage of food, which was a common complaint on British vessels well into the twentieth century. After killing the master and mates during evening prayers, the mutineers changed their ship's name to *Revenge* and turned pirate.

Smith had a short but violent career. He pirated several ships, mainly British, in the seas off Portugal, but was unlucky in his captures. An English ship loaded with cod and a Scots vessel carrying pickled herring were not sufficiently valuable for men hoping for wine or gold, so the pirates began to grow frustrated. At length, the supplies on *Revenge* were eaten, and Smith landed at Madeira, kidnapped the governor and, threatening him with death, obtained provisions for his ship.

The next capture was an English slaver, which they robbed before putting their prisoners on board. When Smith decided that a French vessel was too powerful to fight, one of the crew, a man named Williams, called him a coward, and attempted to shoot him. Williams was promptly captured and locked up. He was later put aboard a Bristol vessel that Smith had robbed. By now the pirates realised that the authorities would send a warship to capture them and debated their next move. While some hoped to sail to the West Indies, others favoured the American colonies or West Africa, but Smith suggested sailing to Orkney, an out-of-the-way spot where nobody would think of searching. Smith also believed that they could rob the larger houses in the islands with some ease.

Once in an Orcadian bay, Smith spent time with a Manx smuggler and a Swedish ship, but some of the more reluctant of his crew slipped ashore and turned King's Evidence. Meanwhile, Smith began the second part of his plan by sending armed men to plunder the home of Mr Honeyman, the High Sheriff. Another party kidnapped and abused two women, one of whom subsequently died, while Smith led a third to rob a man named Fea. When Smith ran *Revenge* aground, Fea raised the island against the pirates and captured all twenty-eight without losing a man. Guarded by soldiers from Edinburgh, Smith and his crew were shipped to London, where they met their old comrade Williams. Smith, Williams, and six others were hanged, with the others acquitted, as they had only become pirates under duress.

Yet for all the furore caused by pirates, by the

eighteenth-century privateers were much more prolific. There were occasions when privateers of rival nations met. Such an event occurred in 1760 when the Leith ship *Edinburgh*, under the command of Thomas Murray, met a French privateer in the Caribbean. At first, the Frenchman had the advantage, nearly crippling *Edinburgh* with well-aimed broadsides at her rigging, but Murray ordered that all his cannon be manhandled to one side of the ship and waited. Only when the Frenchman closed to board did Murray give the order to fire, but his single volley sent the Frenchman reeling. Unable to chase in his shattered condition, Murray retired to Barbados to refit, knowing that his enemy was severely damaged.

During the American War of Independence, and the French wars at the end of the eighteenth century, shipowners again fitted out their vessels as privateers, partly as a means of retaliation against enemy vessels, but also to make profits. As the American war hit, the Clyde tobacco companies' hard, fourteen Clydeside vessels were hunting in the Atlantic in the first year. Although privateering could be extremely profitable, the shipowners still had to calculate profit and loss probabilities before deciding whether or not to purchase a Letter of Marque. The cost depended on the size of the ship, with a ship with over 150 men being charged a whopping £3000, but only half that for a smaller vessel. It was no wonder that most privateers were relatively small vessels that haunted known sea lanes.

On top of the licence fee, the shipowner, or more often consortium of shipowners, also had to buy offensive armament. If the privateer hoped to land a precious prize, she had to be prepared to fight, for the larger merchant vessels, such as Indiamen, were all well-armed. The shipowner had to balance the weight of armament against the speed of his craft, for every side in wartime used convoys, which would be defended by warships that could outgun all but the largest and most expensive of privateers. Only the unwary, the coaster or the fast 'runner' vessels would be out alone.

Adding to the shipowners' problems was the cost of the provisions. A privateer had to carry a large crew to enable her to man the vessels that she captured, and each man had to be adequately fed and watered for a voyage that might last weeks or even months. Food was expensive in a country at war, as were insurance rates, which always rose alarmingly. Lastly was the wages bill. Knowing their value, merchant seamen were higher paid in wartime, and unless the shipowner agreed on a 'no purchase, no pay' contract, the privateer crew would demand a fair day's wage for a fair day's plundering. Even if the privateer were lucky, the Crown would take one-sixth of the profit, and the crew another quarter. The shipowner was left to make a profit from the remainder.

Some, however, did just that. One notable Clydeside vessel was *Lady Maxwell* of Port Glasgow. Commanded by William Gilmour, the long, lean craft carried only ten guns but was so adept a hunter that the French knew her as the 'scourge of the Channel.' It was on a January morning, with the mist coiling above the surging seas off Ushant that *Lady Maxwell* had her closest scrape. With brandy casks filling her holds, Gilmour peered through the fog, searching for the two French schooners that were expected at any time. At length, the lookout cried 'Sail ho!'

'What ship?' Gilmour bellowed and blinked when the reply came.

'*Alliance*, in the squadron of Captain John Paul Jones!'

Clapping on all sail, Gilmour sped away. His 10-gun privateer would be no match for a squadron of American and French vessels.

Of all the Clydeside shipowners, it was the Glasgow tobacco lords—the merchants who dominated the tobacco trade between Scotland and North America—that invested most heavily in privateers. During the American war, the Clyde fitted out thirty-seven privateers, but so successful was the Royal Navy in blockading the enemy coasts that they captured only forty-seven prizes. In 1781 the Glasgow merchants, Speirs, French and Company fitted out *Enterprise*, who boldly sailed out and captured a brace of enemy ships. Despite selling ships and cargo for £1,200, Speirs, French lost money on the adventure. Other companies had better luck. For instance, the ship *Cochrane*, owned by William Cunningham and Company, brought home a French East Indiaman whose cargo of Oriental spices and silks realised a colossal £100,000. *Cochrane* also captured three American vessels in 1778, but most Scottish ships hunted for the French, who had many more ships at sea, and whose cargoes were usually more valuable. One Clydeside schooner, with the apt name of *Endeavour*, sailed out with ten diminutive three-pound cannon, saw a much larger French vessel looming through the night and closed for the kill.

After a quick broadside and a call to surrender, Endeavour sent a prize crew on board the Frenchman, who lowered his flag before realising just how small the Clyde ship was.

The sugar port of Greenock also readied a handful of privateers with 'a Letter of Marque and Reprisal and bound on a cruise against the American rebels and for the apprehending and Taking the Ships, vessels and goods belonging to the French King.' Only a few days after leaving the Clyde, Elizabeth captured a pair of French West Indiamen. *La Victoire* and *Beauvoisin* carried sugar and coffee, with their combined cargoes realising over £12,000. However, not all the Clyde vessels actively hunted for prizes; many carried Letters of Marque as a standby. If they happened to come across a weaker enemy ship, they would legally capture her.

Captain Smith sailed in *Sally*, one of these lightly armed part-privateers in 1777 and was sufficiently fortunate to capture a French vessel off St Kitts in the Caribbean. After gloating over his luck, Smith prepared to sail the prize to a British held port but was surprised by an American privateer. Too weak to fight and too heavily laden to take on more cargo, Smith scuttled the French ship and fled before the privateer captured him.

As early as 1777 Boston alone had twenty-one privateers at sea, with every other port in the rebellious colonies eager to add their quota to the total. Indeed at one stage, there were so many privateers in commission that the United States Navy had to resort to press-gang tactics to raise crews. Excellent seamen, many with knowledge of the British coastline and delighting in twisting the lion's tail, the American privateers proved a dangerous enemy. They were fortunate as Britain had a vast merchant fleet that sailed in every ocean and a navy that was overstretched.

In 1777 the Scottish Conventions of Royal Burghs asked for Royal Naval assistance against 'the alarming depredations made by rebel privateers.' In response, the Navy sent HMS *Arethusa*, which cruised the North Channel between Ireland and Scotland, but shipping in the Clyde still felt threatened, particularly when there were fears of an enemy landing in Scotland. So alarmed were some coastal communities that in July the people of Ayr carried their 'valuable furniture' inland. Some might have seen the American privateers swarming offshore, for in June that year they captured fourteen Clydeside vessels.

Although privateers carried armaments such as swivels and carriage guns, Scotland was gaining a reputation in the armament industry for its carronades. Built at Carron near Falkirk, they were lightweight and had a short range that made them suitable for defending against privateers that liked to close and board.

There were at least two recorded instances when Scottish vessels armed with carronades fought off privateers. The first was in August 1778 when Captain John Hastie repelled a French privateer, and the second when an American privateer attacked *Sharp* of Glasgow off Cape Clear, south west Ireland. The carronades were so effective that the master declared he 'intended never to arm with anything else in the future.' However effective carronades might be, there was still the problem of American privateers in the Firth of Clyde.

Alarmed at the loss of trade and profit, the merchants of Greenock, Glasgow, and Port Glasgow clubbed together and fitted out three privateers purely to defend the Clyde and Irish Sea. 'We hope soon,' the merchants declared, 'to be able to protect our trade without the assistance of government, who, it seems, cannot spare us any frigates at present.'

Collecting a hundred seamen from the quays and taverns of the Clyde, the merchants armed them and, according to the Scots Magazine, 'the sailors' were 'so keen…that in case of calm weather they are taking plenty of oars on board.'

However, the privateers were not totally successful. The three vessels, *Charming Fanny*, *Katie*, and *Ulysses*, put out to search for American privateers. Katie was the first to sight a sail, but her master did not investigate. Simultaneously, *Charming Fanny* was forced back into port, leaving only two vessels on patrol. Ulysses then hailed an English vessel, but rather than being reassured, the Englishman believed she was an American and threw the ship's papers into the Clyde. *Ulysses* accompanied her into port, to explain the situation and ensure no genuine Americans were waiting to pounce. Other merchant vessels saw the Scottish privateers and fled in fear, some nearly running aground in their panic. Ignoring such

PIRATES AND PICKLED HEADS

manifestations of nervousness, *Ulysses* and *Katie* berthed at Belfast to seek news of any Americans.

The Irishmen proved suspicious of these alien ships and promptly arrested the master and officers of both, only releasing them when they were confident of their purpose. By that time, an American rabble-rouser had raised a mob that attacked the Scots, who had to flee the port. Overall, Scottish privateers had a mixed war, but the experience would be valuable when the next conflict came along, as it did in 1793.

Although mariners could not know, they were entering the final years of privateering. In some ways the French wars of 1793 to 1815 were the last times great fleets of sailing vessels would hunt the seas, and privately-owned ships would hunt for plunder on behalf of king or government. The old days were coming to an end in a blaze of blood and glory.

THE LAST HURRAH—
REVOLUTION AND A CHINESE
SCOTSMAN

Although piracy has not died, and probably will always survive in some form or another, it is unlikely that Scottish privateers will ever take to the sea again. However, when the French Revolutionary War began in 1793, shipowners sighed at the inevitable increase in insurance rates, merchant seamen tightened their belts and devised methods of evading the press-gang, and many men rubbed their hands at the prospect of prize money. Once again it was time for privateers to sail from the Forth, the Tay, and the Clyde.

The Royal Navy was stretched to the limit, defending Britain's trade across five oceans. At that time, the French and their allies could put out countless privateers, from hundreds of European ports and creeks. Although many naval officers scorned privateers, any help was welcome in the struggle with Revolutionary and Napoleonic France.

There were occasions when Scottish merchant ships proved able to fight off privateer attacks. In 1802 the Edinburgh and Leith Shipping Company first began their regular runs to London. They used smacks, cutter-rigged, sailing vessels, and carried arms, for the East Coast of Britain was as dangerous in the early nineteenth-century as it was to become during the 1940s. It was October 1804 when *Britannia* of the Edinburgh and Leith Company was sailing off Cromer in company with an English vessel named *Sprightly*. When a large ship approached, they became suspicious, and when the stranger opened fire the masters of the smacks knew that it was a French privateer. As the Frenchman's cannonballs holed their sails and sliced through their rigging, both smacks replied with their carronades, sending the privateer running to seek an easier victim.

Scottish privateers, however, continued to trawl the seas for prizes. One of the most daring was *Roselle* of Leith, a 14-gun vessel who battled yardarm to yardarm with French or Spanish ships. Arriving in Peterhead one day, her master fired a cannon to wake the town, but so alarmed a Greenland whaler that her master clapped on all sail and fled out to sea. *Roselle*, however, was more bold than sensible, for she strayed too close to a Spanish battleship, whose broadsides blasted her out of the water.

The Clyde privateers were also busy. Captain Fraser Smith's *Neptune* sailed to southern waters and captured the French Indiaman *Charles Maurice* on her passage home from Mauritius. Although Fraser Smith and his men did the bloody work of battle and capture, it was Walter Ritchie, owner of Neptune, who gained the bulk of the £25,000 prize money. With that success behind her, *Neptune's* next voyage was to the Pacific coast of South America, where she mingled general trade with a hunt for pirates until a brace of Spanish warships captured her. Privateering was a roller-coaster business of ups and downs, grand success, or spectacular disaster.

Despite the wide-ranging adventures of Scottish privateers, home waters remained as dangerous as ever.

In October 1808, the sloop *James and Margaret* of Montrose, with Andrew Craigie as master, was sailing north about from Newcastle to Liverpool. She hit stormy weather in the Pentland Firth and put into Wideawake Bay for shelter. This time it was a Danish privateer who cut her out, leaving the master and crew on shore at Hoy but carrying away the vessel as a prize. By 1813 the Americans were again the enemy, and an American schooner privateer was hovering off Cape Wrath, capturing small vessels and waiting for the homeward bound whaling fleet. No seas were safe, despite the vigilance of the Navy.

With the end of the Napoleonic and American Wars in 1815, the days of European privateers were virtually over. As long as warships and merchant vessels were similar in style and design, privateering was possible, but throughout the nineteenth century, warships developed along new lines. They became much more specialised, faster, with armour plate, and rotating gun turrets, so that only a costly conversion could create a fighting vessel from a merchantman. Recognising the fact, a European convention signed the Declaration of Paris in 1856, which outlawed privateering. The United States, mindful of the part its privateers had played in the wars with Britain, refused to sign and suffered accordingly when British-built Confederate privateers ravaged Federal shipping in the war between the States.

Privateering, however, was perhaps more distinct from piracy than it had ever been before, and the nineteenth century saw a resurgence of the ancient practice. The last Scottish pirate execution was in 1822 when two sea robbers were hanged at Leith. Nevertheless, Scottish mariners were no angels and tended to turn up in the most unlikely of places. For instance in 1821 *Jane* of Gibraltar, with a crew that included Scots, was bound from Gibraltar to Brazil when the crew mutinied and took over the ship. They sailed to the old pirate island of Barra, where the local customs officer promptly placed them in custody. The ghost of MacNeil would surely have mocked such milk-and-water piracy.

Captain James Hossack of *Henry*, a Kirkcaldy vessel, was sailing from Buenos Aires in November 1826 when he was boarded by a 14-gun Columbian privateer. Rather than burn, loot, and destroy, Captain Pablo Ortiz of *La Guayro* paid Captain Hossack $50 for provisions and let him on his way. It seemed that a new breed of polite pirates was on the seas.

However, Scottish seamen had not lost the old, adventurous spirit. Toward the second half of the nineteenth century, a Glasgow vessel was sailing in the South China Sea when a fleet of junks approached. Perhaps the Glasgow ship was becalmed, for the junks closed and boarded, led by a brawny, particularly ugly looking individual. As the Scottish crew gathered together, expecting to fight for their lives but knowing that they were hopelessly outnumbered, the Chinese looked around the ship and left without taking anything.

The evil looking leader paused before he returned to his own vessel. Summoning the master of the Scottish ship, he smiled and said: 'remember me to any enquiring friends at the Clune Brae foot.' It seems that he was from Port Glasgow on the Clyde, but Chinese pirates had captured him many years previously. Faced with the choice of death or joining the pirates, he had selected the latter and in time rose to be their captain. It is not impossible that there are others like him, even now.

Today piracy is revived and as ugly and dangerous as ever, off the coast of Africa and in other waters. Scottish mariners are still in danger from being boarded, and still must keep a wary eye on the horizon, just in case.

EPILOGUE

So that was something of Scotland's sea history, told in bite-size pieces. It was not an official history, not a continuous history, and certainly did not cover even a hundredth of one per cent of events. It was only a personal view of some of the things that have happened, and a very few of the individuals involved, famous, infamous, and unknown. Every port, every harbour, bay, and island has its quota of stories. Most are forgotten, a few are well-kent, but all should be aired. Scotland was and is a maritime nation; in our time we have spread tartan across the seas of the world.

Helen Susan Swift.

Dear reader,

We hope you enjoyed reading *Pirates and Pickled Heads*. Please take a moment to leave a review in Amazon, even if it's a short one. Your opinion is important to us.

Discover more books by Helen Susan Swift at https://www.nextchapter.pub/authors/helen-susan-swift

Want to know when one of our books is free or discounted for Kindle? Join the newsletter at http://eepurl.com/bqqB3H

Best regards,

Helen Susan Swift and the Next Chapter Team

You might also like:
Strange Tales of Scotland by Jack Strange

To read the first chapter for free go to:
https://www.nextchapter.pub/books/strange-tales-of-scotland-scottish-mysteries

Made in the USA
Monee, IL
24 March 2021